Hostetter, Edwin C.
An elementary grammar
of Biblical Hebrew /

BIBLICAL L

Date Due

St
R

Sheffield Academic Press

An Elementary Grammar of Biblical Hebrew

Edwin C. Hostetter

Biblical Languages: Hebrew

1

Copyright © 2000 Sheffield Academic Press

Published by
Sheffield Academic Press Ltd
Mansion House
19 Kingfield Road
Sheffield S11 9AS
England

http://www.shef-ac-press.co.uk

Typeset by Sheffield Academic Press
and
Printed on acid-free paper in Great Britain
by Bookcraft Ltd
Midsomer Norton, Bath

British Library Cataloguing in Publication Data

A catalogue record for this book is available
from the British Library

ISBN 1-84127-101-2
1-84127-102-0 pa

CONTENTS

PREFACE

The beginning, intermediate and reference grammars in this Biblical Languages: Hebrew series adhere methodologically to a few general guidelines. Consequently, my volume primarily incorporates traditional nomenclature to describe grammatical phenomena. That should make accessible to students commentaries and other resources employing accepted terminology. I do, however, inject certain labels from the field of contemporary linguistics.

The approach taken in this grammar to the order of subject matter is to discuss nouns and particles first and then move on to verbs. Within the verbal category, I address completely strong verbs before paying attention to weak verbs. Thus, roughly one third of the lessons delineate nouns and particles, another third explain strong verbs, and a final third present weak verbs.

In this book I offer examples and exercises that are all culled from the Masoretic Text of the Hebrew Bible. It should be noted that these biblical excerpts, which are intended to serve as both illustration or practice, sometimes display altered punctuation. Likewise, the syntax of these excerpts in isolation does not always duplicate exactly the syntax when they were still embedded in the biblical text.

In Lessons 1 to 24 you will be guided through writing/copying, oral reading, sentence analysis, usage identification, syllable division, parsing and translation. From Lesson 25 you will focus on the last two skills, with a particular emphasis on extended passages of continuous prose and poetry. Annotations are supplied for assistance on points that might pose unusual difficulty. None of the exercises consist of English-to-Hebrew translation. Your performance will entail learning to use a printed Hebrew Bible, a Biblical Hebrew lexicon or dictionary, and an advanced grammar. (When it comes to oral reading, you will be encouraged to imitate modern Israeli sounds for the consonants and vowels. I have attempted to select pronunciation guidewords that are vocalized the same way in both British and American speech.)

The lesson vocabularies contain a total of 230 words, each of which occurs over 170 times in the Masoretic Text; the earliest lessons contain the terms with the highest frequencies. In addition, almost 50 words, such as numerals and pronouns from particular lessons, are inserted into the end-of-book vocabulary list. Verbal paradigms and a subject index accompany this glossary. The introductory overview of how Hebrew fits within the Semitic languages makes reference to several valuable publications.

I wish to thank those who have studied Biblical Hebrew with me across the years: especially China Ashe, Kathryne Ballou, Catherine Barnes, Joan Brown, Roger Cillo, Lucille Coleman, Norman Downs, Michael Hackney, Jebb Jackson, Anthony Kotlar, Arthur Lyons, Rebecca MacEwen, John Markel, Andrew McIntyre, Larry Moon, Jason Park, Mindaugas Puronas, Gregory Seltzer, William Tyler and Karen Wenell. Naturally, my appreciation also goes to the series editor Richard Hess and to the publisher Sheffield Academic Press.

Edwin C. Hostetter
Baltimore, June 1999

INTRODUCTION

Biblical Hebrew is the language of the books of the Hebrew Bible/Old Testament, with the exception of relatively small scriptural portions written in Biblical Aramaic. The Hebrew Bible is a collection of writings whose composition spans most of the millennium from the twelfth century to the second BCE. However, it is important to recognize Biblical Hebrew as a form of the spoken language standardized at a particular time and perpetuated thereafter as a fixed literary medium. It is generally assumed that Biblical Hebrew is a close approximation to the language of the monarchic period preceding the exile of the Jews to Babylon (thus, before 587 BCE). The comparatively sparse inscriptional material of the ninth to seventh centuries corroborates this view. We may suppose that Biblical Hebrew ceased being nourished by living dialects after the Babylonian exile.

Hebrew, though restricted by Greek and Aramaic, continued to be spoken across Palestine in a style called Middle or Mishnaic or New Hebrew until the Bar-Kokhba revolution against Roman rule resulted in the devastation of Judaea (132–35 CE). Biblical Hebrew itself, now a dead language, has always been used as a literary medium and constitutes one of the most important components of Modern Hebrew as revived in Israel.

Hebrew belongs to the northwest branch of the extensive subfamily of languages named Semitic after a traditional ancestor, Noah's son Shem. Together with such languages as Phoenician and Moabite, Hebrew constitutes the northwest branch's Canaanite division. Other northwest Semitic languages include Aramaic and Ugaritic. The remaining two principal branches of the Semitic subfamily are northeast (Akkadian, comprising Babylonian and Assyrian) and south (Arabic and Ethiopic).

Modern printed versions of the Hebrew Bible derive from several essentially similar sources, all reflecting the grammatical activity in Tiberias of Jewish traditionalists, who by the tenth century CE had

perfected a system of vowel notation and added it to the received consonantal text. This standard Hebrew Bible is known as the Masoretic
Text. The current edition of the Masoretic Text used by most students
and scholars is to be found in Karl Elliger and Wilhelm Rudolph (eds.),
Biblia Hebraica Stuttgartensia (Stuttgart: Deutsche Bibelstiftung,
1967–77) (*BHS*). A critical apparatus displaying variant readings supplements the printed scriptural text. Norman Henry Snaith (ed.), *Hebrew Old Testament* (London: British & Foreign Bible Society, 1958) is
a handy edition which omits any critical apparatus. The following three
books will be of aid in your use of modern Hebrew Bibles, especially
that edited by Elliger and Rudolph: (1) William R. Scott, *A Simplified
Guide to BHS* (North Richland Hills, Texas: BIBAL Press, 3rd edn,
1995); (2) Reinhard Wonneberger, *Understanding BHS: A Manual for
the Users of 'Biblia Hebraica Stuttgartensia'* (trans. Dwight R. Daniels;
Subsidia Biblica, 8; Rome: Editrice Pontificio Istituto Biblico, 2nd rev.
edn, 1990); (3) Ernst Würthwein, *The Text of the Old Testament: An
Introduction to the Biblia Hebraica* (trans. Erroll F. Rhodes; Grand
Rapids: Eerdmans, 1995).

As hinted earlier, this and other grammars of Biblical Hebrew deal
with what is primarily a written language. The standard reference grammar is currently Paul Joüon, *A Grammar of Biblical Hebrew* (trans. and
rev. Takamitsu Muraoka, Subsidia Biblica, 14; Rome: Editrice Pontificio Istituto Biblico, 1991). Nevertheless, A.E. Cowley (ed.), *Gesenius'
Hebrew Grammar* (Oxford: Clarendon Press, 2nd English edn, 1910)
remains a valuable tool. Two works on the narrower subject of syntax
are J.C.L. Gibson, *Davidson's Introductory Hebrew Grammar—Syntax*
(Edinburgh: T. & T. Clark, 4th edn, 1994) and Bruce K. Waltke and
Michael O'Connor, *An Introduction to Biblical Hebrew Syntax* (Win-
ona Lake, IN: Eisenbrauns, 1990). Once you have progressed beyond
the elementary phase of learning the language, you may wish to acquire
Ehud Ben Zvi, Maxine Hancock and Richard Beinert, *Readings in Biblical Hebrew: An Intermediate Textbook* (Yale Language Series; New
Haven: Yale University Press, 1993) or J.H. Eaton (ed.), *Readings in
Biblical Hebrew* (University Semitics Study Aids, 3–4; 2 vols.; Birmingham: University of Birmingham, 1976–78).

The two best lexicons of Biblical Hebrew currently available are
David J.A. Clines (ed.), *The Dictionary of Classical Hebrew* (8 vols.;
Sheffield: Sheffield Academic Press, 1993–), and Ludwig Koehler,
Walter Baumgartner and Johann Jakob Stamm, *The Hebrew and*

Aramaic Lexicon of the Old Testament (trans. M.E.J. Richardson; 5 vols.; Leiden: E.J. Brill, 1993–). William L. Holladay, *A Concise Hebrew and Aramaic Lexicon of the Old Testament* (Grand Rapids: Eerdmans, 1971), is basically an abridgement of the latter. Not to be disregarded on account of age is the full-length yet single-volume classic Francis Brown, S.R. Driver and Charles A. Briggs, *A Hebrew and English Lexicon of the Old Testament* (Oxford: Clarendon Press, 1907). When it comes to a concordance for the Hebrew Bible, you can choose from Abraham Even-Shoshan (ed.), *A New Concordance of the Bible* (Jerusalem: Kiryath-Sepher, 2nd edn, 1989); Gerhard Lisowsky and Leonhard Rost, *Konkordanz zum hebräischen Alten Testament* (Stuttgart: Württembergische Bibelanstalt, 1958); or Solomon Mandelkern, *Veteris Testamenti Concordantiae Hebraicae atque Chaldaicae* (ed. Moshe Henry Goshen-Gottstein; New York: Schocken Books, 3rd edn, 1959).

LESSON 1

Alphabet

1.1. The Letters and Their Names

Block Script		Name	Transliteration	Cursive Script	
א		Aleph	ʾ	ⲕ	
ב		Beth	b		
ג		Gimel	g		
ד		Daleth	d		
ה		He	h		
ו		Waw	w	/	
ז		Zayin	z		
ח		Heth	ḥ	ⲛ	
ט		Teth	ṭ		
י		Yod	y		
כ	ך*	Kaph	k		*
ל		Lamedh	l		
מ	ם*	Mem	m		*
נ	ן*	Nun	n		/*
ס		Samekh	s		
ע		Ayin	ʿ		
פ	ף*	Pe	p		*
צ	ץ*	Ṣade	ṣ	3	*
ק		Qoph	q		
ר		Resh	r		
ש (that is, שׂ and שׁ)		Sin and Shin	ś and š	ẹ and ẹˑ	
ת		Taw	t		

[* A special form used at the end of a word.]

1.2. Pronunciation

א	a silent letter, not sounded
ב	with a dot* (בּ), *b* as in 'book'
	without a dot* (ב), *v* as in 'village'
ג	with a dot* (גּ) or without (ג), *g* as in 'go'
ד	with a dot* (דּ) or without (ד), *d* as in 'dark'
ה	*h* as in 'hot'
ו	*v* as in 'village'
ז	*z* as in 'zoo'
ח	*ch* as in the ending of German 'Bach' and Scottish 'loch'
ט	*t* as in 'ten'
י	*y* as in 'yes'
כ	with a dot* (כּ), *k* as in 'keep'
	without a dot* (כ), *ch* as in the ending of German 'Bach' and Scottish 'loch'
ל	*l* as in 'long'
מ	*m* as in 'make'
נ	*n* as in 'now'
ס	*s* as in 'sing'
ע	a silent letter, not sounded
פ	with a dot* (פּ), *p* as in 'pill'
	without a dot* (פ), *f* as in 'finger'
צ	*ts* as in the ending of 'nets'
ק	*k* as in 'keep'
ר	*r* as in 'run'
שׂ	*s* as in 'sing'
שׁ	*sh* as in 'shoe'
ת	with a dot* (תּ) or without (ת), *t* as in 'ten'

[* Explained at Lesson 4.]

1.3. The Writing System

The Hebrew alphabet contains only consonants, not vowels. (Lesson 2 will describe markings used to indicate vowels.)

There is no uppercase and lowercase distinction among Hebrew letters.

Four of the five word-final forms (ך, ן, ף and ץ) extend below the line. The only non-final form to descend below the line is qoph (ק).

Printed matter such as books and newspapers employ the block or square script of the alphabet. The modern cursive script may be found in handwritten materials.

Certain letters may cause confusion due to their having similar form: (1) ב and כ, (2) ג and נ, (3) ד, ך and ר, (4) ה, ח and ת, (5) ו, י and ן, (6) ט and מ, (7) ם and ס, (8) ע, צ and ץ.

Some consonants sound alike: (1) ב and ו, (2) ח and כ, (3) ט and ת/ט, (4) כ and ק, (5) ס and שׂ.

The letters א and ע have no sound at all.

Hebrew is written from right to left so that a word whose consonants are lamedh, mem, daleth would be written למד. This means that words and sentences are read from the right, pages from the top right-hand corner, and books from what we would consider to be the back.

Transliterated Hebrew is written, like English, from left to right. No system of transliteration or transcription for Biblical Hebrew has been universally adopted. The schema presented in this grammar will be applied by way of illustration to the vocabulary words in Lessons 2 to 4.

Exercises

1. Memorize the sequence of the Hebrew consonants—both their forms and names. (In other words: א, ב, ג...שׂ, שׁ, ת, + aleph, beth, gimel...sin, shin, taw.) Practice writing the shape of each letter at least two or three times. Say the names of the letters aloud.

2. Utter the sound that every consonant makes, according to the pronunciation guide above.

3. Copy each of the following words and then 'spell' it by recording the names of the letters: e.g., למד = lamedh, mem, daleth.

ישׂראל	היה
אלהים	ארץ
יהוה	לא
עשׂה	כי
מלך	בן

LESSON 2

Vowels

2.1. Signs, Names and Sounds

Sign	Name	Transliteration
_	pataḥ	a
ָ	qāmeṣ (*namely* qāmeṣ gādôl/rāḥāb)	ā
ֶ	s^egōl	e
ֵ	ṣērê	ē
ֵי	ṣērê yōd	ê
ִ	ḥireq	i
ִי	ḥireq yōd	î
ָ	qāmeṣ qāṭān/ḥātûp	o
ֹ	ḥōlem	ō
וֹ	ḥōlem waw	ô
ֻ	qibbûṣ	u
וּ	šûreq	û
ְ	š^ewâ	^e
ֲ	ḥāṭēp pataḥ	^a
ֱ	ḥāṭēp s^egōl	^e
ֳ	ḥāṭēp qāmeṣ	^o

Many grammarians choose to classify pataḥ, s^egōl, ḥireq, qāmeṣ qāṭān, and qibbûṣ as short vowels and qāmeṣ gādôl, ṣērê or ṣērê yōd, ḥireq yōd, ḥōlem or ḥōlem waw, and šûreq as long vowels. The transliterative marks above correlate with that division: long vowels with macron or caret, short vowels without diacritics.

2.2. *Pronunciation**

ְ, pataḥ and ָ, qāmeṣ (gādôl or rāḥāb), *a* as in 'raj'.

ֶ, sᵉgōl and ֵ, ṣērê and ֵי ṣērê yōd, *e* as in 'they'.

ִ, ḥireq and ִי, ḥireq yōd, *i* as in 'machine'.

ָ, qāmeṣ qāṭān (or hātûp) and ֹ hōlem and וֹ, hōlem waw, *o* as in 'bone'.

ֻ, qibbûṣ and וּ, šûreq, *u* as in 'flute'.

ְ, simple šᵉwâ and compound šᵉwâs (ֱ, ḥāṭēp pataḥ and ֳ, ḥāṭēp sᵉgōl and ֳ, ḥāṭēp qāmeṣ), *a* as in 'abut' or *e* as in 'finger' or *o* as in 'vision'. (These four are known as reduced vowels.)

[*For alternative systems of pronunciation for the first twelve (full) vowels, consult the Appendix.]

The combination of certain vowels with the consonant yōd at the end of a syllable—or especially at the end of a word—produces the following four diphthongs: pataḥ + yōd (ַי); qāmeṣ + yōd (ָי) sound like *ai* in 'aisle'; hōlem + yōd (ֹי) or hōlem waw + yōd (וֹי) sounds like *oi* in 'toil'; šûreq + yōd (וּי) sounds something like *uey* in 'gluey'. (When pataḥ + yōd or qāmeṣ + yōd precedes a word-final waw [that is, ַיו or ָיו], the yōd is silent and the vowels are pronounced normally.)

2.3. *The Pointing System*
These vowel signs or 'points' were added to the consonants of the Hebrew Bible during the second half of the first millennium CE—that is, between the sixth and tenth centuries—by a community of scribes known as Masoretes in order to preserve the Jewish tradition of how to read (or utter) the scriptural text.

Most of the vowel signs stand directly below the consonants with which they are read: for example, בַ, בֶ, בִ. However, hōlem waw and šûreq are placed after their consonants (as is of course the yōd in ṣērê yōd and ḥireq yōd): בוֹ, בוּ, בֵי, בִי. Also simple hōlem appears over a letter: בֹ.

In a word where hōlem follows the letter sin, the vowel may be written to coincide with the dot which marks the consonant: thus שֹ—although שׂ is possible too. Likewise in a word where hōlem precedes the letter shin, the vowel may be written to coincide with the dot which marks that consonant: thus שֹ—although again שׁ is possible.

2.4. *Same Sign, Different Sound*
Qāmeṣ and qāmeṣ qāṭān share the same sign: ָ. In Lesson 6.4 the rules for determining which vowel the sign represents in a given word will be

outlined. Until then, read this point consistently as qāmeṣ (gādôl) unless told otherwise.

Vocabulary

אֱלֹהִים	*'ᵉlōhîm*	'God, gods'
אָמַר	*'āmar*	'to say'
בּוֹא	*bô'*	'to come, enter'
בֵּן	*bēn*	'son'
הָיָה	*hāyâ***	'to be, happen'
יהוה	*yhwh*	'Yahweh' (probably spelled originally יַהְוֶה* but revocalized [that is, furnished with new vowels] early on in the Bible as if the word written in the text were really Hebrew אֲדֹנָי ['Lord'] or Aramaic שְׁמָא ['the name'])
כִּי	*kî*	'because, that, when, indeed'
כֹּל	*kōl*	'all, every'
לֹא	*lō'*	'not'
עָשָׂה	*'āśâ***	'to do, make'

[*   The šᵉwâ here, which is silent, will be explained in Lesson 6.3.]
[** Final qāmeṣ hē is often transliterated â instead of āh.]

Exercises

1. Memorize the signs and names of the vowels. (Sequence is unimportant.)

2. Practice writing every vowel point with the letter he. (See several samples with samekh above.) Then sound aloud all sixteen of the syllables that you have just created.

3. Copy the ten vocabulary words and spell them by recording the names of the consonants and vowels. Pronounce each word in the list, stressing/accenting the final syllable. Learn the meanings of the vocabulary items.

LESSON 3

Accents, Pause, Meteg, Maqqēf

3.1. Accents

The majority of Hebrew words are stressed or accented on their final syllable (ultima) although many others are stressed instead on their next to last syllable (penult).* A word's primary stress or accent must fall on one of these two syllables. All of the vocabulary items in Lesson 2 receive ultimate stress. Here are a couple instances from the current lesson's vocabulary which receive penultimate stress: אֶרֶץ and בַּיִת. In this grammar an acute accent symbol (´) will mark any word whose penult is the stressed syllable: for example, מֶ֫לֶךְ (the šᵉwâ is silent just as in יְהִי, which was encountered in the vocabulary list of Lesson 2). Otherwise it may be assumed that the ultima is the stressed syllable.

[*Lesson 6 will elucidate syllabication.]

The same scribes—the Masoretes—responsible for supplying the consonantal Hebrew text with vowel signs also devised a system of accent marks, which were added to the vocalized text. These marks are about equally divided between those written over the letters/consonants and those written beneath. The accent symbols serve three purposes:

1. They indicate which of a word's syllables (either the ultima or the penult) gets the heaviest stress. In a long word there can be an additional accent mark before the penult to indicate a syllable that gets a secondary, lighter stress. (An area of potential confusion is that a few accents [called prepositives] are always positioned at the beginning of a word and a few [postpositives] always at the end, regardless of the syllable to be stressed. One must then determine the stress position through a knowledge of grammar.)

2. They divide a verse into its logical units or constituent parts and show how its sentence structure or syntax was perceived

at the time when the accent symbols were placed into the text of the Hebrew Bible. Hence they aid in interpretation. Disjunctive accents separate verse components; conjunctive accents join verse components. (Concerning conjunctives and disjunctives, see the advice at the end of this section.)

3. They regulate the chanting of the Scriptures in synagogues. Ironically, a synagogue scroll does not show vowels and accents; they are recited from memory.

The two principal accent marks in each verse are sillûq and 'atnāḥ (both disjunctives). Sillûq (̣) occurs below the stressed syllable of a verse's final word, which immediately precedes the verse-ending punctuation called sôf pāsûq (:)—for example, בֹּא׃. 'Atnāḥ (̭) occurs below the stressed syllable of the word that ends a verse's first half—for example, אֱלֹהִ֑ים. Since the two halves of a verse are determined by sense rather than by length, they may vary greatly in length. (For the remainder of the accent symbols—approximately forty in all, depending on how they are counted—one of the reference grammars listed in the Introduction to this grammar should be consulted.)

3.2. *Pause*

Words marked with certain disjunctive accents (especially 'atnāḥ and sillûq) are said to be *in pause*. In the course of reading there is a noticeable halt or break after such words. (This compares with the pause following a comma in modern English.) Because the tendency is to prolong the utterance of words in pause, they often possess a vocalization and even an accentuation slightly different from that of the usual context form.

Examples:*

Nonpausal	*Pausal*	
עַם	עָם	pataḥ shifted to qāmeṣ
אֶרֶץ	אָרֶץ	sᵉgōl shifted to qāmeṣ
וַיֵּלֶךְ	וַיֵּלַךְ	ṣērê shifted to pataḥ
כְּבֵדָה	כָּבֵדָה	šᵉwâ shifted to ṣērê and became stressed
יָדְךָ	יָדֶךָ	šᵉwâ shifted to sᵉgōl and became stressed
תִּשְׁמְרוּ	תִּשְׁמֹרוּ	šᵉwâ shifted to ḥōlem and became stressed
אֲנִי	אָנִי	ḥāṭēp pataḥ shifted to qāmeṣ and became stressed

[*Including words and forms not encountered so far.]

3.3. *Meteg*
The meteg is a short perpendicular stroke (ֽ) placed under a consonant
and usually to the left of a vowel whose pronunciation it restrains: that
is, prevents rapid or accelerated pronunciation. Also, meteg frequently
indicates a word's secondary stress (as a kind of half-accent) and occasionally indicates a word's syllabic division. (Lesson 6 will treat syllables more fully.) Unfortunately neither manuscripts nor grammarians
are in accord regarding the use of meteg. A general rule covering the
most common cases is that meteg may be added to the vowel of the first
open syllable that is removed from the primary stress by at least a nonsilent š°wâ* if not by one or more actual syllables. Here are a variety of
instances illustrating meteg—בֵּית־אֵל וְזָהָב לְמִינֵהֶם אָרְחֹתָיו. (The foregoing general rule does not cover the last example.)

[*All compound š°wâs (that is, ḥāṭēp pataḥ, ḥāṭēp s°gōl, and ḥāṭēp qāmeṣ) are nonsilent. Simple š°wâ can be either nonsilent or silent. Grammarians sometimes refer
to nonsilent š°wâs as 'vocal' or 'mobile'.]

Although meteg looks exactly like sillûq, the two are easily distinguish-
able since the latter appears only on the stressed syllable of a verse's
final word.

3.4. *Maqqēf*
When two or more short words within a verse are closely associated
syntactically, they are sometimes joined together by a hyphen or dash
called maqqēf (־). The phrase בֵּית־אֵל encountered already in the
meteg discussion is an example, as are כִּי־לֹא־טוֹב and קְנֵה־אֹתָנוּ. Words
so connected are read as a single speech unit with the primary stress
falling on the final word in the unit. All other words in the unit lose
their original stress. The loss of an accent before maqqēf may lead to an
adjustment in vocalization (usually a shift from a 'long' vowel to its
corresponding 'short' variety [see Lesson 2.1]). Thus, שֹׁמֵר changes its
second vowel to qāmeṣ qāṭān in שָׁמָר־לְךָ; יָם changes its qāmeṣ (gādôl)
in יַם־סוּף; and אֵת changes its vowel in אֶת־קוֹלִי.

Vocabulary

אִישׁ	'îš	'man, husband'
אֶרֶץ	'ereṣ	'earth, land'
בַּיִת	bayit	'house'
יָד	yād	'hand'

יוֹם	*yôm*	'day'
*יִשְׂרָאֵל	*yiśrā'ēl*	'Israel'
*מֶלֶךְ	*melek*	'king'
נָתַן	*nātan*	'to give, allow, put'
עַם	*'am*	'people'
פָּנִים	*pānîm*	'face'

[*This š^ewâ is silent as in יְהוֶה (cf. Lesson 2).]

Exercises

1. Memorize the vocabulary and continue to do so in subsequent lessons.

2. After turning to 1 Sam. 1.1-5 in a Hebrew Bible (see my resource list in the introduction), copy the two words in every verse that are accented with either 'atnāḥ or sillûq. Then copy all the words marked with a meteg. Finally, copy the units of words linked by maqqēf.

3. Now practice reading aloud these words which you have written. (Please note that in וּלְכָל־ the vowel ָ is qāmeṣ qāṭān. The š^ewâ in the following words is silent: אֶפְרַיִם, אֶלְקָנָה, אֶפְרָתִי, לְהִשְׁתַּחֲוֹת [the middle one of the three only; also the waw is a consonant], רָחְמָה [ignore the dot in the he for now].)

LESSON 4

Dagesh (Lene, Forte, Euphonic)

4.1. *Lene*
In Lesson 1 it was noted that six letters—beth, gimel, daleth, kaph, pe, taw—can be written either with or without a dot. This dot is known as a dagesh: specifically dagesh lene, or weak dagesh. Historically those six consonants were given a hard or plosive pronunciation whenever containing the dagesh lene. Whenever lacking dagesh they were uttered as a soft or fricative sound. Generally only בּ and ב, כּ and כ, פּ and פ are distinguished from each other in the Hebrew speech of modern Israelis. (Observe the pronunciation guide in Lesson 1.2.) A mnemonic device for remembering which consonants sometimes accept a dagesh lene is the artificial phrase בֶּגַד־כְּפַת (Begadkefat).

Dagesh lene normally appears in these consonants when they begin words or when within words they begin syllables not immediately preceded by a vowel (including mobile šᵉwâ). For example, גָּזַל and יִסְפֹּר (with silent šᵉwâ). Dagesh is absent from a so-called Begadkefat letter which is preceded by a vowel. For example, נָבִיא and וְדָרוֹם (with mobile šᵉwâ) and נְחֹשֶׁת. In a sentence the mere fact that the preceding word ends with a vowel is sometimes enough to warrant dagesh's omission from a Begadkefat which begins the next word.

4.2. *Forte*
Dagesh forte, or strong dagesh, occurs in letters to show that they are doubled. Its placement is not limited to the Begadkefat consonants. There are two reasons for the doubling of a letter:

1. Assimilation produces doubling. If a word has another word or an affix joined to it, a letter from the one element can become absorbed into an adjacent letter of the other element. For instance, the preposition מִן ('from') often attaches to the word it governs so as to form a single word. Thus מִן + שָׁאוּל ('Saul')

becomes a hypothetical מִנְשָׁאוּל. However the nun changes its
sound into the sound of shin. Therefore the word is written
מִשָּׁאוּל to indicate the doubled shin after the loss of nun. We
can compare this phenomenon with similar English develop-
ments like 'illegal' resulting from the root 'legal' + the prefix
'in'; the *n* assimilates to the *l*.

2. Certain verbal and nominal patterns require doubling as a
characteristic feature. A sample of the former is הִתְאַמֵּץ (a verb
stem, hithpael, to be introduced in Lesson 24). A sample of the
latter is גִּבּוֹר ('hero', the first dagesh is lene), although these
types of nouns are not extremely abundant.

It should be noted that when a consonant which would normally
demand a dagesh forte is followed by a vocal šᵉwâ, the dagesh can be
omitted in some situations. For example, הַיְלָדִים instead of הַיְּלָדִים; יִשְׂאוּ
instead of יִשְּׂאוּ. Only teth and the Begadkefat letters do not allow for the
omission of doubling under any circumstances.

4.3. *Distinguishing between Lene and Forte*

A source of possible confusion between the dagesh lene and the dagesh
forte is their usage in the Begadkefat. Technically, whenever they represent doubled consonants we should expect two dots in them—one
(forte) to indicate the doubling and another (lene) to indicate the hard or
plosive sound. But since the soft or fricative values for the six Begadkefat letters do not occur doubled, a second dot is superfluous and never
written.

Since both the strong dagesh and the weak dagesh look identical, the
following rule helps to tell them apart: a dagesh in a Begadkefat
consonant will be lene when the letter is not immediately preceded by a
vowel; it will be forte when the letter is immediately preceded by a
vowel. To put it another way, a dagesh lene never stands after a vowel
(for example, בְּרִית) while dagesh forte always does (for example, הַבֵּן).

4.4. *Euphonic*

A special kind of dagesh forte is the euphonic dagesh. Occasionally a
letter in a word is doubled for the sake of clearer or smoother pronunciation. This happens most commonly when a word ending with an
unstressed qāmeṣ or qāmeṣ–he or sᵉgōl–he is followed by a word beginning with a stressed syllable. A dagesh may then be placed in the first
consonant of the second word, for example רָעָה רְע, יָנְקָה־לָּנוּ, הָבָה־לָּנוּ, שָׁבִיתָ שֶּׁבִי.

Vocabulary

אָב	*'āb*	father
דָּבַר	*dābar*	to speak
דָּבָר	*dābār*	word, thing
הָלַךְ *	*hālak*	to go, walk
יָצָא	*yāṣā'*	to go out/forth
יָשַׁב	*yāšab*	to sit, dwell
עִיר	*'îr*	city
רָאָה	*rā'â*	to see
שׁוּב	*šûb*	to turn, return
שָׁמַע	*šāma'*	to hear

[*The šᵉwâ is silent.]

Exercises

1. Turn to Jer. 22.1-5 in the Hebrew Bible. Copy all of the words that contain a dagesh lene. (In every case where a dagesh is in a consonant following a šᵉwâ, it is a silent šᵉwâ—in other words, does not count as a vowel.) Then pronounce each word.*

2. Copy all of the words containing a dagesh forte and utter them aloud.*

[*The first ָ in לְחָרְבָּה (v. 5) is qāmeṣ qāṭān.]

LESSON 5

Gutturals, Mappîq, Rafe

5.1. Gutturals

The gutturals—aleph, he, heth and ayin—and the letter resh possess certain characteristics or features that distinguish them from other letters of the alphabet. (Gutturals are sometimes labelled laryngeals or pharyngeals.) There are three main rules governing the guttural letters:

1. Gutturals and resh cannot be doubled and therefore reject dagesh forte. Instead of the doubling, the vowel before them often undergoes some adjustment. Pataḥ may become qāmeṣ; hireq may become ṣērê; and qibbûṣ may become ḥōlem. This happens less before he and heth than before the rest. For example, the preposition מִן (see the discussion of dagesh lene in Lesson 4.2) + the noun רָע ('evil') produces not מִרַּע but מֵרָע.

2. Gutturals and resh tend to take compound or composite šᵉwâs (that is, the hatefs: ֲ, ֱ and ֳ) rather than simple šᵉwâ (ְ). Ḥāṭēp pataḥ is the reduced vowel used most commonly in such a situation; ḥāṭēp qāmeṣ least commonly. Thus we encounter עֲבֹר rather than עְבֹר; אֱלֹהִים rather than אְלֹהִים; חֲלִי rather than חְלִי. The gutturals' preference for compound šᵉwâs is so great that substitution normally occurs even where the expected simple šᵉwâ would have been silent. In this case the vowel in front of the guttural will be the full-vowel element contained in the hatef found under the guttural. For example, נַעֲמֹד substituted for נַעְמֹד (with silent šᵉwâ).

3. Gutturals and resh favour the vowel pataḥ before them, after them or both. Examples: יְשַׁלַּח instead of יְשַׁלֵּח; וַתַּעַד instead of וַתַּעֵד; נַעַר instead of נַעֵר.
   When a word ends with a guttural preceded by šûreq, ḥōlem/ḥōlem waw, hireq yōd, or ṣērê, a glide vowel (namely, pataḥ)

is generally inserted between the two. In other words, while the extra pataḥ (called 'furtive pataḥ') is written under the final guttural, it is pronounced before it. Furthermore, the sound of the furtive pataḥ does not count as an additional syllable and so never gets stressed. Examples include שִׁיחַ and גְּבֹהַּ. (See the next section for the dot in the he.)

5.2. *Mappîq*

The letter he is usually silent or quiescent when it stands as the consonant which ends a word. There are cases, however, where final he is meant to be pronounced. To indicate this the Masoretes employed a dot—called mappîq—within the letter. For instance, in סוּסָה ('mare') the he is quiescent, but in סוּסָהּ ('her stallion') the he is sharply audible, uttered the same as when located at the beginning of a word.

5.3. *Rafe*

Rafe, which appears above a consonant, expresses the opposite of mappîq and of dagesh (whether forte or lene). In contrast to mappîq, rafe indicates that a final he is not pronounced: for example, לָהֿ. In contrast to dagesh forte, rafe indicates that a letter is not doubled: for example, עֹרִֿים. In contrast to dagesh lene, rafe indicates that a Begadkefat is fricative: for example, פָֿנֶיךָ (the first qāmeṣ is qāṭān). Current printed editions (*contra* manuscripts) of the Bible almost entirely omit the sign for rafe for technical reasons.

Vocabulary

אִם	'if'
דָּוִד	'David'
הִנֵּה	'behold, lo'
יָדַע	'to know'
יְהוּדָה	'Judah'
לָקַח	'to take'
עַיִן	'eye, fountain'
עָלָה	'to go up'
שֵׁם	'name'
שָׁנָה	'year'

[*הִנֵּה can also serve as a predicator of existence, with the meaning 'here is' (or 'here are'). Thus, הִנֵּה זֶבַח (Judg. 8.15) may be rendered 'Here is Zebah'. הִנֵּה־רֹאשׁ (2 Sam. 4.8) may be rendered 'Here is a head'. (Hebrew common nouns are inherently indefinite. Lesson 7 will introduce the definite article.)]

Exercises

1. Translate the following five phrases. Every one begins with הִנֵּה as the predicator of existence. Look up each phrase's second term in a Biblical Hebrew lexicon or dictionary (see the resource list in the Introduction to this grammar). Keep in mind that the vowel points do not figure into the lexicon's alphabetical arrangement. Words are alphabetized only by the consonants—including the helping letters (waw and yōd) in the vowels ִי , ֵ֫י , וֹ, וּ.

   a. הִנֵּה־רִבְקָה (Gen. 24.51)
   b. הִנֵּה אֵלִיָּהוּ (1 Kgs 18.14)
   c. הִנֵּה־אִישׁ (Zech. 6.12)
   d. הִנֵּה נָתָן (1 Kgs 1.23)
   e. הִנֵּה מָקוֹם (Exod. 33.21)

2. Turn to Eccl. 1.1-11 in a Hebrew Bible to observe the three characteristics of gutturals and resh.

   a. For the first characteristic, copy the word in v. 4 whose he has a qāmeṣ (instead of a pataḥ) ahead of aleph; copy the word appearing twice in v. 6 whose He likewise has qāmeṣ ahead of resh; copy the word in v. 9 whose yōd is vocalized with a ṣērê (instead of a ḥireq) ahead of ayin. Pronounce all three terms. (Verse 4's term receives penultimate stress.)

   b. For the second characteristic, copy two words appearing twice in v. 2 that have he + ḥāṭēp pataḥ; copy the two words in v. 3 and the one word in v. 9 whose ayin has that ḥāṭēp pataḥ; copy the word in v. 10 whose aleph is vocalized with ḥāṭēp pataḥ and the two words in v. 11 whose heth is so vocalized. Utter aloud all the terms you have just written.

   c. For the third characteristic, copy the word in v. 3 and the same word in v. 9 whose heth is both preceded and succeeded by a pataḥ; copy the word in v. 5 and the word appearing twice in v. 6 with a furtive pataḥ under its heth; copy the word in v. 8 whose ayin bears the furtive pataḥ. Again practice pronunciation. (The term in vv. 3 and 9 receives penultimate stress.)

LESSON 6

Syllables, Silent Šᵉwâ

6.1. Syllables

With one main exception, a syllable in Hebrew must start with a consonant. That exception to the rule surfaces when a word starts with a šûreq as in וּבֵין. (Lesson 7 will describe this conjunctive waw.) A Hebrew syllable normally includes one and only one full vowel. The number of full vowels in a word consequently determines the number of syllables. In addition to a full vowel, a syllable may contain a reduced vowel (which will stand beneath the consonant beginning the syllable). The half vowel is considered part of that syllable and does not count as a separate syllable. For example: אָבִיו has two syllables, אָ and בִיו; אֲרָצוֹת has two syllables, אֲרָ and צוֹת; בְּרִית has one syllable, בְּרִית; מֵאָדָם has three syllables, מֵ and אָ and דָם.

When calculating syllabification, a letter doubled by dagesh forte always divides in the middle. This does not mean that there is any perceptible pause between the syllables in pronunciation; a doubled letter is simply held longer than a single one. Contrast the longer *n* of English 'meanness' from the shorter *n* of 'any'. Accordingly: הַשָּׁמַיִם has the four syllables of הַשׁ and שָׁ and מַ and יִם; לְבָּךְ has the two syllables of לְב and בָּךְ.

6.2. Open and Closed Syllables

Syllables in Biblical Hebrew are classified as either open or closed. An open syllable may be defined as one that ends in a vowel. A closed syllable is one that ends in a consonant. Syllables containing a diphthong (see the second section of Lesson 2) are to be considered closed, taking the waw or yōd as a consonant. For example: in חַי, the sole syllable is closed; in יִסֹּבּוּ, the first syllable יִ is open but the second סֹב is closed while the third בּוּ is open too; in נַעֲשֶׂה, the first syllable נַ is open and so is the second עֲשֶׂה (remember from last lesson that he at the end of a word quiesces and ceases to function as a letter); in גְּזַל, the first syllable גְּ is open while the second זַל is closed.

6.3. Silent Šᵉwâ

In Lesson 2 it was noted that Hebrew makes use of a silent šᵉwâ—written exactly like the simple vocal šᵉwâ ( ) but serving an entirely different purpose. The silent šᵉwâ stands beneath a letter that ends a syllable and may therefore be referred to as a syllable divider. This means that when a simple šᵉwâ stands beneath a consonant which begins a word, the šᵉwâ is vocal: for example, בְּיָדוֹ. Also a simple šᵉwâ which sits beneath a consonant doubled by dagesh forte will always be vocal: for example, קִטְּרוּ. The same holds for a šᵉwâ under the first of two identical consonants: for example, רוֹמְמוּ. Finally, whenever two šᵉwâs stand under adjacent letters within a term, the first šᵉwâ will be silent while the second vocal: for example, תִּשְׁמְרוּ and אֶבְחֲרָה.

How does a person determine in other instances, however, whether a simple šᵉwâ is silent or vocal? Here are a pair of guidelines addressing the majority of situations:

1. When the šᵉwâ is preceded by a pataḥ, sᵉgōl, hireq, qāmeṣ qāṭān or qibbûṣ (customarily known as short vowels), the šᵉwâ is silent and ends a syllable: for example הִשְׁכַּב and יִגְלֶה.
2. Elsewhere the šᵉwâ begins a syllable and is vocal*: for example יוֹשְׁבִים and זִיתְךָ.

[*This is not true of course when the šᵉwâ appears in a final kaph. When used as the final letter, kaph routinely bears a raised šᵉwâ sign if it lacks any other vowel, for example: הִשְׁלִיךְ.]

6.4. Qāmeṣ Gādôl or Qāmeṣ Qāṭān?

In Lesson 2.4 it was noted that the vowel sign ָ can represent either qāmeṣ gādôl or qāmeṣ qāṭān. When ָ occurs alongside a šᵉwâ a number of rules help to differentiate between the two types of qāmeṣ:

1. If the sign precedes a letter bearing both simple šᵉwâ and dagesh forte, it will be qāmeṣ qāṭān: for example, בְּעָזְּךָ. So too if the sign precedes two consonants, each pointed with šᵉwâ: for example, כָּתְפְשְׁכֶם.
2. On the other hand, before a pair of identical consonants where šᵉwâ sits underneath the first, the vowel sign ָ indicates qāmeṣ gādôl: for example סָבְבוּ. Likewise whenever the syllable with the sign is stressed: for example, לָיְלָה.

3. Should none of these conditions prevail, it is possible to discern the vowel intended solely by learning vocabulary words as well as nominal and verbal inflectional patterns. (Sometimes manuscripts and printed editions place meteg next to such a vowel sign to clarify its representing qāmeṣ gādôl; but this is by no means standard practice.)

When simple šᵉwâ does not reside under a letter which follows the ֽ sign, our decisions are easier: qāmeṣ qāṭān is found in unstressed closed syllables: for example, חָנֵּי. Qāmeṣ gādôl is found in the other types of syllables—stressed closed, stressed open, unstressed open:* for example, קָם, וַיָּשֶׂם and כָּבוֹד respectively.

[*But not in front of ḥāṭēp qāmeṣ, where ֽ equals qāmeṣ qāṭān: for example, נָעֳמִי.]

Vocabulary

	אָדוֹן	'lord, master'
	אַיִן*	'nothing'
	אָכַל	'to eat'
	אִשָּׁה	'woman, wife'
	גַּם	'also, even'
לֵב (or לֵבָב)		'heart'
	מֹשֶׁה	'Moses'
	עֶבֶד	'servant'
	שָׁלַח	'to send'
	שָׁם	'there'

[*Just as הִנֵּה can serve as a predicator of existence, even more so אַיִן (in the special construct form אֵין to be learned about in Lesson 11) can serve as a predicator of nonexistence, with the meaning of 'there is/are not'. Thus, אֵין־דָּבָר (Num. 20.19) may be rendered 'there is not a word' or 'there is no word'.]

Exercises

1. Translate the following five phrases. Every one begins with אֵין, the predicator of non-existence. In a lexicon look up the definition of each phrase's second term.

   a. אֵין חֵקֶר (Isa. 40.28)
   b. אֵין חֵפֶץ (Jer. 22.28)
   c. אֵין חָזוֹן (1 Sam. 3.1)
   d. אֵין־קֵץ (Isa. 9.6)
   e. אֵין מִסְפָּר (Gen. 41.49)

2. Turn to Psalm 15 in the Hebrew Bible. Copy every word con-
    taining any kind of qāmeṣ. Identify in them every šᵉwâ (silent
    or vocal) and qāmeṣ (qāṭān or gādôl) using the rules outlined
    above. Divide these words into syllables. Pronounce all the
    terms out loud.

LESSON 7

Article, Waw Conjunction, Interrogatives

7.1. Article
In the vocabulary section of Lesson 5 it was observed that Biblical Hebrew has no indefinite article (that is, 'a' or 'an' in English). It is the absence of the definite article (that is, 'the' in English) that indicates a word's indefiniteness. Thus יוֹם—minus the article—may be translated either 'day' or 'a day'.

The article never stands alone but attaches to the front of the term whose definiteness it determines. Its basic form is הַ + the doubling of the following consonant. For example, לֵב with the article becomes הַלֵּב; נַעַר with the article becomes הַנַּעַר.

The article of Hebrew corresponds closely to the definite article of English in usage and meaning. Thus הַיּוֹם signifies 'the day.'

7.2. Other Forms of the Article
The article has a slightly different form when prefixed to a word whose initial letter is resh or a guttural (aleph, he, heth, ayin), since these letters refuse to be doubled (see Lesson 5.1).

1. Before he and heth the article is usually pointed הַ without a succeeding dagesh forte: for example, הַהֵיכָל and הַחֹשֶׁךְ.
2. Before aleph, ayin, and resh, the article is normally written הָ—again the dagesh forte is absent: for example, הָאָב, הָעִיר, הָרָעָב.
3. Before a word whose first syllable is הָ unstressed, חָ (whether stressed or not), or עָ unstressed, the article will be הֶ and the following consonant will lack dagesh forte: for example, הֶעָפָר הֶחָכָם, הֶחָיִל, הֶהָרִים and.

A dagesh after the article is regularly omitted from yōd (for example, הַיְשׁוּעָה), frequently omitted from mem (for example, הַמְכַסֶּה), and occasionally omitted from other nonguttural consonants (for example, הַלְוִיִּם).

Finally, several terms modify their appearance under the influence of the article. Here is a list:

הַר becomes הָהָר	אֶרֶץ becomes הָאָרֶץ	אֲרוֹן becomes הָאָרוֹן
פַּר becomes הַפָּר	עַם becomes הָעָם	חַג becomes הֶחָג

7.3. *Waw Conjunction*

The conjunction וְ, 'and', is prefixed to a succeeding word, whose initial consonant determines the form of the waw conjunction. It is important to become familar with the following rules:

1. Ordinarily waw conjunction is pointed with šᵉwâ: for example, וְהָאָדָם, וְסוּס.
2. Before a letter bearing a simple šᵉwâ and before beth, mem, or pe, the conjunction waw becomes וּ: e.g., וּנְקֵבָה, וּפֹה.
   An exception occurs if a term starts with יְ, in which situation the elements contract: for example, וְ + יְהִי produce וִיהִי.
3. Preceding a guttural vocalized with a compound šᵉwâ, the conjunction takes the full vowel corresponding to that reduced vowel: for example, וַאֲנִי.
   However, the opening aleph in the word for deity loses its ḥāṭēp sᵉgōl, and the vowel under the waw becomes ṣērê: that is, וֵאלֹהִים. The divine name יהוה presents a similar special instance. Instead of reading אֲדֹנָי (see the vocabulary list in Lesson 2) after the conjunction, the aleph quiesces so that we sound the consonants ויהוה as וַאדֹנָי and not וַאֲדֹנָי.
4. Immediately before a stressed syllable, the pointing often appears as וָ— especially in word pairs: for example, וָמָתְנוּ, טוֹב וָרָע.

7.4. *Interrogatives*

Any sentence may be converted into a simple yes-or-no question by prefixing the interrogative he to the first word. The customary pointing for the particle is הֲ (for example, הֲזֶה from זֶה). Again, the pointing of the prefix depends on the succeeding consonant:

1. In front of a guttural—but not resh—supported by a qāmeṣ gādôl or a ḥāṭēp qāmeṣ, the form is הֶ (for example, הֶאָנֹכִי from

אָנֹכִי). Consequently it could look like the definite article when preceding stressed הָ and unstressed הָ, הַ or עֲ.

2. Before gutturals supported by all other vowels and before any consonant followed by a šᵉwâ besides ḥāṭēp qāmeṣ, the interrogative particle is pointed הַ (for example, הַאִין from אִין; הֲמִעַט from מְעַט). It could therefore look the same as the article prior to he or heth.

An example from translation helps to illustrate the effect of interrogative he: שַׂמְתָּ equals 'You placed' while הֲשַׂמְתָּ equals 'Did you place?'

7.5. *Interrogative Pronouns and Adverbs*

Questions may be introduced by interrogative pronouns and adverbs.

מָה—which refers to things and means 'what?'—sometimes stands alone but more often joins the following word by way of maqqēf. The vocalization of this interrogative is similar to although less consistent than the article:

1. Before ordinary letters (excluding gutturals and resh), the form is מַה + a doubling of the next word's first consonant: for example, מַה־יָּפִית.

2. The pronoun is also written מַה, but without dagesh forte, in front of heth and he (except when that he is the article): for example, מַה־הוּא. aleph, ayin and resh generally take מָה: for example, מָה אַרְצֶךָ. However, when he, heth, and ayin have the vowel qāmeṣ—or sometimes even a different vowel—the interrogative is spelled מֶה: for example, מֶה־עֲוֹנִי.

מִי—which refers to people and means 'who?'—usually stands alone but occasionally joins the following term via maqqēf. The vocalization of this interrogative pronoun does not vary: for example, מִי עָשָׂה.

Common interrogative adverbs, which may introduce questions, include:

אַיֵּה or אֵי; also אֵיפֹה	'where?'
אֵיךְ or אֵיכָה	'how?'
מַדּוּעַ	'why?'
מָתַי	'when?'

It is important to note that unlike those found in English, Hebrew clauses (whether statements or questions) can assume a linking verb without its being specified. A couple of translative illustrations, using the foregoing pronouns and adverbs will help to clarify:

1. The second word (reading right to left) in מִי הָאֲנָשִׁים (Num. 22.9) means 'the men', so that we render the whole clause 'Who are the men?'.

2. The second term in אַיֵּה שָׂרָה (Gen. 18.9) means 'Sarah', so that we render the entire phrase 'Where is Sarah?'

For each sentence we must supply the linking verb 'are' and 'is' respectively.

Vocabulary

אַל	'not'
דֶּרֶךְ	'way'
יְרוּשָׁלַיִם	'Jerusalem'
כֹּהֵן	'priest'
מוּת	'to die'
מִצְרַיִם	'Egypt'
נֶפֶשׁ	'soul, person'
נָשָׂא	'to lift, carry'
קוּם	'to rise, stand'
קָרָא	'to call, read'

Exercises

1. Several of the following words bear the (definite) article; several do not. Employ the rules above to tell which is which. Then pronounce them all aloud (only qāmeṣ qāṭān, not gādôl, goes before a simple šᵉwâ in this list).

הֲדַסָּה	הִגְלַת	הַגּוֹאֵל	הַבָּנִים	הָאִישׁ
הִתְבָּרְכוּ	הֶעָרִים	הֶעֱמִיד	הַמָּצָא	הַחֲלוֹם

2. Read aloud and on paper translate these clauses, looking up each second term (some of which may have the article here).
   a. אַיֵּה יהוה (2 Kgs 2.14)
   b. אֵיפֹה שְׁמוּאֵל (1 Sam. 19.22)
   c. מַה־זֶּה (Est. 4.5)
   d. מִי־הָאִישׁ (Ps. 34.13)
   e. מָתַי קֵץ (Dan. 12.6)

LESSON 8

Prepositions, Object Marker, He Directive

8.1. Prepositions
From a purely formal point of view Hebrew has three types of prepositions: (1) those joined directly onto the following word and written as part of it; (2) those written as separate words; and (3) one that may appear either way.

Inseparable Prepositions
The prepositions בְּ, 'in' or 'by', כְּ, 'like' or 'as', and לְ, 'to' or 'for', are called inseparable. They have no existence as separate words but like the waw conjunction attach themselves as prefixes to the terms they govern. These prepositions are normally vocalized with a šᵉwâ: for example, בְּעִיר.

Before a consonant which has a simple šᵉwâ, the šᵉwâ under the preposition becomes a ḥireq since two šᵉwâs cannot stand together at the beginning of a word: for example, כִּפְרִי. However, this is not the case if the preposition is prefixed to a term whose initial consonant supported by šᵉwâ is yōd. Then the resultant ḥireq beneath the preposition combines with the yōd to produce ḥireq yōd, and the simple šᵉwâ drops out: for example, לִיהוּדָה.

When attached to a word whose first letter is a guttural supported by a composite (that is, compound) šᵉwâ, an inseparable preposition assumes the corresponding full vowel: for example, כַּחֲלוֹם, בַּחֲלִיִּים and לֶאֱמֶת. Exceptions may occur before an aleph with a ḥāṭēp sᵉgōl, where the preposition infrequently receives a ṣērê and the compound šᵉwâ falls away: for example, לֵאמֹר. Likewise, the combination of the tetragrammaton יהוה and a preposition, כיהוה for example, is pronounced as כַּאדֹנָי and not כַּאֲדֹנָי. (See the vocabulary list in Lesson 2.)

Sometimes immediately in front of the tone (that is, stressed) syllable, the vowel of the preposition becomes qāmeṣ (gādôl): for example, בָּאֵלֶּה.

Finally, when inseparable prepositions join words containing the (definite) article, the he of the article disappears and surrenders its vowel to the preposition: for example, בַּבְּרִית from a hypothetical בְּהַבְּרִית.

Independent Prepositions

The most common unattached or independent prepositions are:

אַחֲרֵי/אַחַר	'after'		לִפְנֵי	'before'
אֶל	'toward'		עַד	'until'
אֵת	'with'		עַל	'upon'
*בֵּין	'between'		עִם	'with'
לְמַעַן	'for the sake of'		תַּחַת	'under'

[*With each element of a compound prepositional phrase בֵּין is repeated: for example, בֵּין הָאוֹר וּבֵין הַחֹשֶׁךְ is rendered 'between the light and the darkness' (Gen. 1.4).]

Often, yet often not, the independent prepositions unite with the succeeding terms by maqqēf (in which case אֵת becomes אֶת־): for example לִפְנֵי שַׁחַת, אֶל־מָחוּץ and עַל שֵׁם.

The Preposition מִן

The preposition מִן, 'from', generally combines with the word it precedes. Its customary punctuation (that is, vocalization) is ḥireq with the nun assimilating to the next letter, which is then doubled: for example, מִיּוֹם. Contraction occasionally takes place when the word coming after מִן starts with י: for example, מִירוּשָׁלַיִם rather than מִיְרוּשָׁלַיִם.

Ahead of terms whose initial consonant is a guttural or resh, the preposition joins directly as the form מֵ—for example, מֵרֹאשׁ.

When followed by the article, the preposition can remain separate (with or without maqqēf) or can become inseparable: for example, מֵהַמֶּלֶךְ, מִן הָעֵץ.

Prepositions with Interrogatives

The inseparable preposition לְ + the interrogative pronoun מָה produce לָמָּה, 'why?' or literally 'for what?'. Before the gutturals aleph, he and ayin the form לָמָה—with ultimate or final stress—is preferred.

The preposition מִן + the interrogative adverb אַי (through some further modification) result in מֵאַיִן, 'whence?' or literally 'from where?'.

8.2. *Object Marker*

When the direct object of a verb (this will be discussed in Lesson 14 onwards) has the article, that object is very commonly preceded by the particle אֵת or (with maqqēf) אֶת־. This is true also when the direct object is a proper name. An indefinite word seldom takes the particle: for example: אֵת הַשָּׁמַיִם, where שָׁמַיִם as the object of a transitive verb bears the article; אֶת־דָּוִד, where דָּוִד as the direct object is a proper name.

Since the Hebrew sign אֵת/ אֶת־ serves merely to draw attention to the object, it is never translated into any corresponding English term. (Observe how the direct object marker looks exactly like the preposition אֵת/ אֶת־. Context will distinguish between them.)

8.3. *He Directive*

The suffix הָ added to a term mainly indicates motion toward something. This he directive/he locale occurs on adverbs (for example, שָׁמָּה 'thither', from שָׁם 'there') and proper nouns (for example, בָּבֶלָה 'toward Babylon', from בָּבֶל 'Babylon') and common nouns—with or without the article (for example, הַמִּדְבָּרָה or מִדְבָּרָה 'to the/a wilderness', from מִדְבָּר 'wilderness'). Sometimes vowel changes take place: for example, קֵדְמָה 'eastward', from קֶדֶם 'east.' The directive he syllable in a word never receives the stress/accent.

Note that אָנָה 'whither?', apparently possesses the הָ particle attached to אָן 'where?'.

Vocabulary

אָדָם	'human beings'
אָח	'brother'
בַּת	'daughter'
גּוֹי	'nation'
הַר	'mountain'
כֹּה	'so, thus'
כֵּן	'so, thus'
מַיִם	'water'
רֹאשׁ	'head'
שִׂים	'to place'

Exercises

1. Translate the following prepositional phrases (for example,
   מֵאֶרֶץ 'from a land'):

אֶל־יְרוּשָׁלַיִם	מִבַּת
בֵּאלֹהִים	עַד־הָעֶרֶב
כְּאָדָם	עַל הַכִּסֵּא
לְמַעַן צִיּוֹן	עִם־הָעָם
לִשְׁמוּאֵל	תַּחַת גֶּפֶן

2. Translate these six words containing the directional he (which,
   remember, can cause vowel alteration to the original word):

אַרְצָה	הָעִירָה	הַשָּׁמַיְמָה
יְרוּשָׁלַיְמָה	שְׁאוֹלָה	הַבַּיְתָה

LESSON 9

Nouns

9.1. Gender

Hebrew nouns are either masculine or feminine. There is no neuter gender. Nouns referring to animate beings usually have grammatical gender corresponding to natural gender (sex): for example, בֵּן 'son', is masculine; בַּת, 'daughter', is feminine. Otherwise gender is metaphorical. Rivers and water tend to be masculine; countries and cities tend to be feminine. So too terms denoting body parts which exist in pairs are generally feminine. But there are many unclear correlations between gender and meaning: for example, הַר 'mountain', is masculine; גִּבְעָה 'hill', is feminine. And some words may be used as either masculine or feminine.

Nouns ending in accented/stressed הָ or in ת will ordinarily be feminine: for example, צָרָה and דְּמוּת.* However, there are exceptions: for example, קֹהֶלֶת is masculine. Nouns without those endings will normally be masculine: for example, סוּס and נָבִיא. Again, there are exceptions: for example, אָחוֹן is feminine. A word's gender becomes known to us mainly through its agreement with adjectives (to be taught in the next lesson).

[*You will recognize, therefore, that לַיְלָה (with unaccented הָ) is masculine. Furthermore, since the feminine termination הָ always receives the tone while the directional termination הָ (see the discussion of he directive in Lesson 8.3) never receives the tone, you can avoid confusing the two.]

9.2. Number

Three categories of number are distinguished in Biblical Hebrew— singular, dual and plural. The dual is very restricted in use, being found primarily with paired parts of the body and with set expressions of time and number. Sometimes a dual noun is extended to have a plural meaning: for example, יָדִים routinely signifies 'two hands' but in certain contexts may signify 'hands' (that is, more than two). Not all singular words have a matching dual or even plural: for example, singular שֶׁמֶשׁ, 'sun'. Similarly, not all duals or plurals have a matching singular: for example, dual מֹאזְנַיִם 'scales, balance'; plural מְתִים 'men'.

Duality and plurality are marked by special endings. The dual termination for both the masculine and the feminine is ־ַיִם: for example, שְׂפָתַיִם from שָׂפָה;* יוֹמַיִם from יוֹם. (שָׁמַיִם 'sky', and מַיִם 'water', are not duals but abnormal plurals.)

[*A transformation of word-final he into taw before suffixes is common, as are vowel alterations earlier in words receiving suffixes—exemplified by šᵉwâ replacing qāmeṣ.]

Most masculine nouns have plurals ending with ־ִים, while most feminines with וֹת (or ־ֹת): for example, עֵצִים from עֵץ; תּוֹרוֹת from תּוֹרָה.*
There are however several exceptions, including the particularly interesting אָבוֹת from אָב 'father', and רְחֵלִים from רָחֵל 'ewe'. A few nouns can display either plural form: for example, both עֲבֹתִים and עֲבֹתֹת from עֲבֹת.

[*Notice that here (and in similar cases) the feminine indicator ־ָה disappears instead of the he becoming taw.]

9.3. *Nominal Patterns*
Unfortunately, many plurals (as well as duals) are not formed by simply adding these special endings to singular nouns, but the singular nouns themselves frequently undergo changes in the presence of such additions. Discussion follows of commonly encountered patterns for masculine and feminine singular nouns which are modified prior to forming plurals.

1.   Some single-syllable words with two consonants will double the second consonant before plural terminations; when this happens the vowel may undergo changes: for example, חַג becoming חַגִּים, צַד becoming צִדִּים, יָם becoming יַמִּים, עֵת becoming עִתּוֹת, חֹק becoming חֻקִּים.
     Gutturals and resh, of course, reject dagesh forte: for example, שַׂר becoming שָׂרִים, אָח becoming אַחִים.
     (Monosyllables which are altogether irregular include: בַּת becoming בָּנוֹת, בֵּן becoming בָּנִים, אִישׁ becoming אֲנָשִׁים, עִיר becoming עָרִים, יוֹם becoming יָמִים, רֹאשׁ becoming רָאשִׁים [here

the aleph has quiesced and behaves as if totally absent].)

2. Some two-syllable nouns with a closed and accented final syllable (see Lesson 6) possess vowels in the first syllable which undergo no alteration when the plural components are suffixed. However, the second vowel (not counting silent šᵉwâ) might alter: for example, אֶצְבַּע becoming אֶצְבָּעוֹת, מִזְבֵּחַ becoming מִזְבְּחוֹת, סֵפֶר becoming סְפָרִים.* Or still different alterations could occur: for example, חַטָּאת becoming חַטָּאוֹת, מַלְכוּת becoming מַלְכֻיּוֹת, מָגֵן becoming מָגִנִּים.

Other comparable two-syllable nouns will alter their first vowel: for example, דָּבָר becoming דְּבָרִים, זָקֵן becoming זְקֵנִים, אָסִיר becoming אֲסִירִים, מָקוֹם becoming מְקוֹמוֹת, בָּחוּר becoming בַּחוּרִים, לֵבָב becoming לְבָבוֹת. Although the second vowel normally stays the same, observe גָּמָל becoming גְּמַלִּים.

[*The glide vowel, furtive pataḥ (see the discussion in Lesson 5.1), abandons a guttural in the middle of a word.]

3. Plurals in a group of (generally disyllabic) terms bearing the tone on the penult exhibit vowels which have shifted from the singular: for example, מֶלֶךְ becoming מְלָכִים, מִשְׁמֶרֶת becoming מִשְׁמָרוֹת, סֵפֶר becoming סְפָרִים, בֹּקֶר becoming בְּקָרִים; note also גֹּרֶן becoming גְּרָנוֹת, קֹדֶשׁ becoming קָדָשִׁים (with qāmeṣ qāṭān in syllable one), אֹהֶל becoming אֹהָלִים.* Since the last vowel in the singular form is sᵉgōl, this group is often called sᵉgōlate nouns. In reality, however, when a guttural is the final letter, it is preceded by a pataḥ; when a guttural is the next to final letter, it is preceded and succeeded by a pataḥ. No different effect is felt on the plurals: for example, זֶבַח becoming זְבָחִים, אֹרַח becoming אֳרָחוֹת, נַעַר becoming נְעָרִים.

(A related irregular noun is דֶּלֶת becoming דְּלָתוֹת.)

[*In מִשְׁמֶרֶת the feminine indicator ת and its preceding sᵉgōl both fall away.]

A similar group of terms bearing penultimate stress has a middle consonant of waw or yōd. That middle consonant customarily turns into a helping vowel letter: for example, זַיִת becoming זֵיתִים, אָוֶן becoming אוֹנִים, but חַיִל becoming חֲיָלִים. (Strangely irregular is בַּיִת becoming בָּתִּים, with qāmeṣ gādôl.)

4. Several singular nouns conclude with הָ, which vanishes in front of a plural ending: for example, מַחֲנֶה becoming מַחֲנוֹת, רֹעֶה becoming רֹעִים.

5. The majority of feminine singular nouns ending in הָ show no change (except for deleting that feminine ending) before a plural suffix: for example, שָׁנָה becoming שָׁנִים, בְּהֵמָה becoming בְּהֵמוֹת, מִשְׁפָּחָה becoming מִשְׁפָּחוֹת. Exceptions to this rule include: אָמָה becoming אֲמָהוֹת, מֶרְכָּבָה becoming מַרְכָּבוֹת. (Observe also the *masculine* פֵּחָה becoming פַּחוֹת.)
(The irregular אִשָּׁה becoming נָשִׁים calls for attention here.)
A subset of feminine nouns with הָ have a simple or compound šᵉwâ under their second letter prior to the he. They make plurals like the sᵉgōlates above: for example, נַחֲלָה becoming נְחָלוֹת, שִׂמְלָה becoming שְׂמָלֹת, חֶרְפָּה becoming חֲרָפוֹת. Exceptions are: מִצְוָה becoming מִצְוֹת, חָכְמָה becoming חָכְמוֹת.*

[*Waw is a consonant rather than a helping vowel letter in מִצְוֹת.]

Vocabulary

גָּדוֹל	'great'
טוֹב	'good'
*(הִכָּה Hiphil) נָכָה	'to smite'
עָבַר	'to pass over'
עוֹד	'again, still'
עָמַד	'to stand'
פֶּה	'mouth'
צָבָא	'army'
*(צִוָּה Piel) צָוָה	'to command'
קוֹל	'voice, sound'

[*Throughout the lesson vocabularies in this volume, if a verb shows in brackets a non-qal stem (Lessons 14 and 21–24 will teach the implied concepts), then that verbal root never appears in the Bible as a qal form—that is, the form outside the brackets.]

Exercises

1. Assuming that the following six words abide by the rules about form and the clues about meaning stated earlier, specify which are masculine and which feminine (with a lexicon's assistance).

מַעֲלֶה	אֵם
צִידוֹן	כְּסוּת
רֶגֶל	מָטָר

2. For these regular plural nouns (i.e., they fit one of the patterns aforementioned), figure out their singular equivalents—again consulting a dictionary.

נְבִיאִים   בְּגָדִים

מַעֲשִׂים   מְלָכוֹת

אֹסֹת   סוּפוֹת

3. Remembering to insert the appropriate form of the English verb 'to be' between the two halves of each clause (see the comment in Lesson 7.5), translate:

a. מַטְמֹנִים בַּשָּׂדֶה* (Jer. 41.8)

b. הַיְּדֹות בֶּעָרִים (Neh. 11.1)

c. שִׁמְעִי מִירוּשָׁלַיִם (1 Kgs 2.41)

d. הַנֶּשֶׁר בַּשָּׁמַיִם (Prov. 30.19)

e. עָפָר מִן־הָאֲדָמָה (Gen. 2.7)

[*For some terms, when their vowels are written in a scriptural passage without a helping waw or yōd, the dictionary headwords may still be spelled with a vowel letter in place (and vice versa: although written with waw or yōd in a text, the term as a lexical entry may in certain cases appear without).]

LESSON 10

Adjectives

10.1. *Gender and Number*
In comparison with other languages, Hebrew has a very limited number
of adjectives. Of those adjectives which do exist, some have a monosyllabic base form: for example, דַּל, רֵיק. However, most are disyllabic:
for example, נָכְרִי, פִּסֵּחַ, בָּצוּר, עָנָו.

Like nouns, adjectives inflect for gender and number. The base form
is used for the masculine singular. For the feminine singular, a qāmeṣ
followed by a he is added to the base form. A ḥireq yōd + a Mem
attaches to the base form to produce the masculine plural. The feminine
plural results from a ḥōlem waw and a taw being appended to the base
form. The adjective טוֹב is inflected as follows:

טוֹב (masculine singular)	טוֹבִים (masculine plural)
טוֹבָה (feminine singular)	טוֹבוֹת (feminine plural)

It should be noted that not all four forms are attested in the Bible for all
adjectives. For instance, the recurrent רָשָׁע, 'guilty', shows no feminine
plural form in Scripture. Moreover, צַדִּיק, 'righteous', appears as only
masculine singular and masculine plural.

10.2. *Declensional Changes*
Also like nouns, adjectives often experience an alteration in the vocalization of their base form before these suffixes. Monosyllabic adjectives
with a pataḥ generally double the second consonant when inflectional
endings are attached—unless that final letter is a guttural or resh, in
which case pataḥ converts to qāmeṣ to compensate for the fact that a
dagesh forte cannot be inserted:

עַז	עַזָּה	עַזִּים	עַזּוֹת
רַע	רָעָה	רָעִים	רָעוֹת

Disyllabics with a qāmeṣ gādôl in the first syllable replace that qāmeṣ with a šᵉwâ when the feminine and plural suffixes are added. When the first consonant is a guttural, however, the qāmeṣ gādôl changes to ḥāṭēp pataḥ.

זְקֵנוֹת	זְקֵנִים	זְקֵנָה	זָקֵן
חֲכָמוֹת	חֲכָמִים	חֲכָמָה	חָכָם

If the last syllable of a disyllabic comprises a consonant followed by a sᵉgōl and a he, the sᵉgōl–he combination drops out in front of the inflectional suffixes:

קָשׁוֹת	קָשִׁים	קָשָׁה	קָשֶׁה

Finally, the adjective קָטֹן behaves irregularly before gender and number endings, in that the pataḥ substitutes for ḥōlem and the nun doubles:

קְטַנּוֹת	קְטַנִּים	קְטַנָּה	קָטֹן

10.3. Attribution and Predication
An adjective functions by qualifying or modifying a noun and may be used in either an attributive or predicative way.

Attributive Adjectives
An attributive adjective joins up with the noun it describes to constitute a phrase which plays a single role in the sentence. (An English illustration would be how the adjective–noun phrase 'friendly dog' functions together as the verb's direct object in the sentence 'We petted a friendly dog'.) Attributive adjectives in Hebrew normally follow their nouns and agree with them in definiteness (see Lesson 7.1), gender and number. For example:

בַּיִת חָדָשׁ	'a new house' (Deut. 22.8)
הַמֹּפְתִים הַגְּדֹלִים	'the great signs' (Deut. 29.2)
אֲרָצוֹת רַבּוֹת	'many lands' (Jer. 28.8)
הַחוֹמָה הָרְחָבָה	'the broad wall' (Neh. 3.8)

Note that an adjective agrees with the gender, not the form, of a preceding noun. This means that even when the endings of nouns are irregular, the endings of adjectives remain consistent and uniform: for example, עִיר גְּדוֹלָה rather than עִיר גָּדוֹל.

Predicative Adjectives
A predicate adjective is juxtaposed to a noun which acts as the subject of a sentence. In such a sentence the linking verb 'to be', though not written, is implied by context and must be supplied in translation. A predicate adjective will agree with the gender and number of its subject noun but will lack the (definite) article, whether the noun bears the article or rarely does not. While subject nouns may stand before or behind predicate adjectives, it is more common for the adjective to precede the noun:

טוֹב־יְהוָה   'Yahweh is good' (Ps. 145.9)

Note that the maqqēf is optional. Observe further, as hinted already in Lesson 8.2, that proper names are to be considered definite in spite of the fact that they do not take the article.

הַיְלָדִים רַכִּים   'The children are tender' (Gen. 33.13)

A pair of predicate adjectives—or for that matter a pair of attributive adjectives—can modify one noun: for example, גּוֹיִם רַבִּים וַעֲצוּמִים 'numerous and mighty nations' (Deut. 7.1); זָקֵן הָאִישׁ וְכָבֵד 'The man was old and heavy' (1 Sam. 4.18). (See from the construction here how the subject noun may split the two adjectives.)

10.4. *Other Adjectival Usage*
The adjective is not altered in form to express the comparative degree. Instead, the preposition מִן (suggesting *difference*) is used ahead of the noun which becomes the basis of comparison: for example,

מַה־מָּתוֹק מִדְּבַשׁ   'What is sweeter than honey?' (or literally, 'What is sweet from honey?') (Judg. 14.18).

Adjectives, usually with the definite article, can behave substantively like nouns and designate 'the one who is...': for example, הֶחָכָם = 'the one who is wise', or 'the wise person'. Evidently the masculine and feminine singular of some adjectives may be used as abstract nouns meaning 'that which is...': for example, רַע and רָעָה for 'wickedness'.

Vocabulary

יָלַד	'to bear, beget'
מָצָא	'to find'
מִשְׁפָּט	'judgment'

נָפַל	'to fall'
עוֹלָם	'eternity'
עַתָּה	'now'
קֹדֶשׁ	'holiness'
רַב	'much, numerous'
שָׁמַיִם	'heaven(s)'
שָׁמַר	'to guard, observe'

Exercises

1. Translate these five clauses/phrases.

    a. מִזָּהָב חֵן טוֹב (Prov. 22.1)

    b. שָׁנָה תְמִימָה (Lev. 25.30)

    c. יוֹם מַר (Amos 8.10)

    d. הַנַּעֲרָה יָפָה (1 Kgs 1.4)

    e. דָּוִיד זָקֵן (1 Chron. 23.1)

2. Each phrase/clause in the column on the right contains a synonym or an antonym for one of the adjectives in the column on the left. Circle every synonym or antonym in the right column and draw a line from it to its correspondent in the left column. Use a lexicon where helpful.

    a. גָּדוֹל   בְּמַיִם עַזִּים (Neh. 9.11)

    b. חָזָק   וְכַתְּאֵנִים הָרָעוֹת (Jer. 24.8)

    c. טוֹב   וְלִפְנֵי עִוֵּר (Lev. 19.14)

    d. פִּקֵּחַ   עֵנָה קְטַנָּה (1 Kgs 17.13)

    e. רָחוֹק   קָרוֹב הַמֶּלֶךְ (2 Sam. 19.43)

LESSON 11

Construct

11.1. *Role and Function of the Construct State*
Nouns and some adjectives in Hebrew actually manifest two so-called
states: absolute and construct. The singular absolute state is the form in
which nouns and adjectives are entered in lexicons or vocabularies. The
dual and plural shapes of nouns and adjectives as learned in Lessons 9
and 10 also display the absolute state. The modifications to appearance
which the construct state typically experiences will be examined later.

Since no preposition exists in Biblical Hebrew which has the same
range of meaning expressed by the English all-purpose preposition
'of ', the construct state helps to fill the gap. The genitival relationship—namely, the various nuances associated with the English preposition 'of '—has its Hebrew correspondent in the construct chain. A
simple juxtaposition of two nouns serves to mark a qualifying relationship and makes up a single combined idea. The first word in such a
chain occurs in the construct state (that is, in a bound form) while the
second occurs in the absolute state (that is, in a free form). Examples
will help to illustrate:

אֲחֻזַּת־קֶבֶר	'a possession of a tomb' (Gen. 23.4)
טְמֵא־שְׂפָתַיִם	'impure of lips' (Isa. 6.5)
יְמֵי עֻזִּיָּהוּ	'the days of Uzziah' (Isa. 1.1)

In the Hebrew Bible the word in the construct state usually bears a
conjunctive accent (mentioned in Lesson 3.1 but not printed in this
volume) and at times precedes a maqqēf, as illustrated by the first two
examples offered above.

A construct chain occasionally extends to three nouns but rarely four or
more. Only the final word in such a series remains in the absolute state:
for example, מִשְׁמַר בֵּית שַׂר הַטַּבָּחִים 'the custody of the house of the
captain of the guard' (Gen. 40.3).

A bound form need not be repeated in front of an additional free form in a compound phrase: for example, the bound form קֹנֵה does not have to be inserted again before the second free form, אֶרֶץ, in קֹנֵה שָׁמַיִם וָאָרֶץ 'maker of heaven and earth' (Gen. 14.19).

11.2. *Qualifying the Construct Chain*
A noun in the construct state never takes the article. The definiteness of the entire chain depends on whether the word in the absolute state is definite or indefinite. (Observe that a noun is considered definite when it has the article or is a proper name [compare Lesson 8.2].)

בַּעַל הַחֲלֹמוֹת   'the owner of the dreams' (Gen. 37.19)

מֹאזְנֵי צֶדֶק   'scales of justice' (Lev. 19.36)

In order to express explicitly 'an X of the Y', the preposition לְ is used between absolute forms of words: for example,

נָבִיא לַיהוָה   'a prophet of Yahweh' (2 Chron. 28.9).

If an adjective modifies any of the nouns in a construct chain, the adjective comes after the whole expression. Some ambiguity might arise about which noun the adjective truly qualifies, but the general context or agreement in gender and number normally serves as a sufficient guide. Thus, in בֶּן־הָאִשָּׁה הַזֹּאת 'the son of this woman' (1 Kgs 3.19) זֹאת (feminine) must modify אִשָּׁה (feminine) instead of בֵּן (masculine).

Multiple adjectives can modify one of the nouns:

כְּלֵי בֵית הָאֱלֹהִים הַגְּדֹלִים וְהַקְּטַנִּים   'the great and small vessels of the house of God' (2 Chron. 36.18) (both of the last two words qualify the initial word).

Although a rough translation employing 'of' often suffices for the meaning of a construct chain, a different preposition or an adjective will really be better in many instances:

הַר קֹדֶשׁ   'a holy mountain' rather than 'a mountain of holiness' (Ezek. 28.14)

סֵתֶר זֶרֶם   'a shelter against rain' rather than 'a shelter of rain' (Isa. 32.2)

11.3. *Nouns and Adjectives in the Construct State*

The construct form of a noun or adjective frequently differs from the absolute state. The feminine singular ending הָ adjusts to ת: for example, שִׂמְחָה becoming שִׂמְחַת. Both the dual and masculine plural endings, יִם and ים respectively, adjust to י: for example, אָזְנַיִם becoming אָזְנֵי and כֹּהֲנִים becoming כֹּהֲנֵי. The feminine plural ending וֹת stays unchanged: for example, רוּחוֹת; the masculine singular has no ending to change: for example, עַם.

In addition to the changes that take place at the end of a word, many words exhibit other vowel changes. Two rules account for the majority of situations:

1. Whenever the first vowel is qāmeṣ or ṣērê in an open un-stressed syllable, there is a tendency for the vowel to be replaced by either a simple or composite šᵉwâ.

   > כְּלִי becoming כֵּלִים   אֲבוֹת becoming אָבוֹת
   >
   > שְׁנַת becoming שָׁנָה

   Exceptions do occur:

   > הֲרֵי becoming הָרִים   עָרֵי becoming עָרִים
   >
   > רָאשֵׁי becoming רָאשִׁים   צָרַת becoming צָרָה

   If, however, the replacement of qāmeṣ or ṣērê creates a situation whereby a vocal šᵉwâ would sit immediately prior to another šᵉwâ, a full vowel replaces this vocal šᵉwâ:

   > עֶדְרֵי becoming עֲדָרִים   נִבְלַת becoming נְבֵלָה
   >
   > (not עֲדְרֵי)   (not נְבְלַת)
   >
   > נַעֲרֵי becoming נְעָרִים   אָרְחוֹת becoming אֲרָחוֹת
   >
   > (not נְעֲרֵי)   (not אֲרְחוֹת)
   >
   > (בְּרֵכַת becoming בְּרֵכָה shows irregularity)

2. In most instances, qāmeṣ—sometimes ṣērê—will become pataḥ when found in a closed stressed syllable. For example: הֵיכַל becoming הֵיכָל. (Routinely, though, בֶּן becomes בֶּן and sporadically שֵׁם becomes שֶׁם.)

   The following examples illustrate that the two rules can operate together:

   > לְבַב becoming לֵבָב   זְקַן becoming זָקֵן
   >
   > חֲכַם becoming חָכָם

A number of less common patterns are also found:

מוֹת becoming מָ֫וֶת   עֵין becoming עַ֫יִן

מִשְׁפַּ֫חַת becoming מִשְׁפָּחָה   מַחֲנֵה becoming מַחֲנֶה

כָּתֵף becoming כָּתֵ֫ף

Totally unpredictable forms include:

אֵ֫שֶׁת becoming אִשָּׁה   אֲבִי becoming אָב

אֲחִי becoming אָח   אֲחֵי becoming אַחִים

One can gain certainty about the correct construct form of a particular noun or adjective only by consulting a dictionary or concordance.

Vocabulary

זָהָב	'gold'
חֶ֫רֶב	'sword'
יָם	'sea'
כֶּ֫סֶף	'money, silver'
מִזְבֵּחַ	'altar'
מָקוֹם	'place'
נָא	'please'
שַׂר	'leader, official'
שָׁאוּל	'Saul'
תָּ֫וֶךְ	'midst'

Exercises

1. Open a Hebrew Bible at Genesis 12. Find the following words in the absolute (or free) state which are preceded by an adjective or noun in the construct (or bound) state. Place that construct adjective or noun in the appropriate blank.

   a. Verse 11: מַרְאֵה _____

   b. Verse 15: פַּרְעֹה _____

                  פַּרְעֹה _____

   c. Verse 17: אַבְרָם _____

                  שָׂרִי _____

2. Now figure out from the rules what the free form of each bound form is. Remember how either a šᵉwâ or a pataḥ could have supplanted either a qāmeṣ or a ṣērê. Look up all words in a lexicon and translate each phrase.

LESSON 12

Demonstratives, Numerals

12.1. *Demonstratives*

A demonstrative adjective or pronoun is one which indicates some person(s) or some thing(s) being singled out for attention. Demonstratives have the following forms:

singular	זֶה 'this' (masculine)	זֹאת 'this' (feminine)
plural	אֵלֶּה 'these' (common = both masculine and feminine)
singular	הוּא 'that' (masculine)	הִיא 'that' (feminine)
plural	הֵם / הֵמָּה 'those' (masculine)	הֵנָּה 'those' (feminine)

Demonstrative adjectives function parallel to attributive adjectives and therefore agree in number, gender and definiteness with the nouns which they limit. Of course, in most such cases the nouns will be definite and the demonstratives will bear the article. After all, by definition a demonstrative identifies an item distinguished from others similar. Examples help to illustrate:

הַיּוֹם הַזֶּה	'this day' (Est. 1.18)
בָּעֵת הַהִיא	'at that time' (Zeph. 1.12)
הַיּוֹם הַהוּא	'that day' (Job 3.4)
לָעֲצָמוֹת הָאֵלֶּה	'to these bones' (Ezek. 37.5)

The demonstrative regularly stands last in a series of adjectives. Examples:

הָאָרֶץ הַטּוֹבָה הַזֹּאת	'this good land' (Deut. 4.22)
הַמֹּפְתִים הַגְּדֹלִים הָהֵם	'those great wonders' (Deut. 29.2)

The form of the demonstrative without the article has the status of a pronoun. Like predicate adjectives, demonstrative pronouns do not take the article but do agree in gender and number with the nouns to which they refer:

Examples:

אֵלֶּה תּוֹלְדוֹת פָּרֶץ   'these are the descendants of Perez' (Ruth 4.18)

הֲזֹאת נָעֳמִי   'Is this Naomi?' (Ruth 1.19) (notice the interrogative particle)

12.2. Cardinal Numerals

Cardinal numbers are used in simple counting or in answer to the question 'how many?'. The table below shows the cardinal numerals from 1 to 10.

Masculine			Feminine	
absolute	*construct*		*absolute*	*construct*
אֶחָד	אַחַד	1	אַחַת	אַחַת
שְׁנַיִם	שְׁנֵי	2	שְׁתַּיִם	שְׁתֵּי
שָׁלֹשׁ	שְׁלֹשׁ	3	שְׁלֹשָׁה	שְׁלֹשֶׁת
אַרְבַּע	אַרְבַּע	4	אַרְבָּעָה	אַרְבַּעַת
חָמֵשׁ	חֲמֵשׁ	5	חֲמִשָּׁה	חֲמֵשֶׁת
שֵׁשׁ	שֵׁשׁ	6	שִׁשָּׁה	שֵׁשֶׁת
שֶׁבַע	שְׁבַע	7	שִׁבְעָה	שִׁבְעַת
שְׁמֹנֶה	שְׁמֹנֶה	8	שְׁמֹנָה	שְׁמֹנַת
תֵּשַׁע	תְּשַׁע	9	תִּשְׁעָה	תִּשְׁעַת
עֶשֶׂר	עֶשֶׂר	10	עֲשָׂרָה	עֲשֶׂרֶת

Naturally the construct state of each numeral precedes the word it qualifies. The absolute state may come before or after. The states can be used interchangeably, with little or no difference in meaning. Numbers 1 and 2 will agree in gender with their associated nouns. Numbers 3 to 10, however, will consistently disagree: that is, masculine forms modify feminine nouns; feminine forms modify masculine nouns:

שְׁאֵלָה אַחַת   'one request'(1 Kgs 2.16)

שְׁלֹשָׁה בָנִים   'three sons' (Gen. 29.34)

שְׁנֵי הַמְּאֹרֹת הַגְּדֹלִים   'the two great luminaries' (Gen. 1.16) (here an attributive adjective supplements the phrase)

Number 11 appears as either עָשָׂר אַחַד or עַשְׁתֵּי עָשָׂר with masculine nouns and either אַחַת עֶשְׂרֵה or עַשְׁתֵּי עֶשְׂרֵה with feminine, while 12 also shows two forms with masculine nouns—שְׁנֵים עָשָׂר or שְׁנֵי עָשָׂר—and two with feminine—שְׁתֵּי עֶשְׂרֵה or עֶשְׂרֵה שְׁתֵּים. For 13 to 19, when modifying masculine nouns the absolute forms of the units are placed before עָשָׂר; when modifying feminine nouns the construct forms of the units are placed before עֶשְׂרֵה. Thus, חֲמִשָּׁה עָשָׂר represents 15 with the masculine and שְׁבַע עֶשְׂרֵה represents 17 with the feminine.

Apart from 20—עֶשְׂרִים—which is the plural of עֶשֶׂר, the tens are plurals of their corresponding units. Thus, תִּשְׁעִים represents 90. Tens do not inflect with gender. Intermediate numbers between 20 and 100 are expressed by uniting tens and units by means of the conjunction waw. The unit, which may come first or second in the compound, correlates in gender with a qualified noun. Thus, both שִׁשִּׁים וּשְׁנַיִם and שְׁנַיִם וְשִׁשִּׁים can be used for 62; similarly, שְׁמֹנִים וַחֲמִשָּׁה and חָמֵשׁ וּשְׁמֹנִים both represent 85. (Only the last of these four specimen illustrations would go alongside a feminine noun.)

Above 99 we encounter מֵאָה, 100; מָאתַיִם, 200; אֶלֶף, 1000; אֲלָפַּיִם, 2000. Hundreds and thousands beyond those will join units to מֵאוֹת and אֲלָפִים respectively. Thus, שְׁלֹשׁ מֵאוֹת is used to express 300; שֵׁשֶׁת אֲלָפִים represents 6000.* Hundreds and thousands do not vary their gender.

[*Constituents higher than 10 prefer אֶלֶף so that שְׁלֹשִׁים אֶלֶף = 30,000.]

One way 2172 could look is אֲלָפַּיִם מֵאָה שִׁבְעִים וּשְׁנַיִם.

It is important to note that nouns attached to numerals from 11 upwards can occur in the singular: for example, אַרְבַּע־עֶשְׂרֵה שָׁנָה 'fourteen years' (Gen. 31.41).

12.3. *Ordinal Numerals*
Ordinal numbers are used for the order of succession in which items are considered. The following chart displays ordinal numerals.

masculine		feminine
רִאשׁוֹן	first	רִאשׁוֹנָה
שֵׁנִי	second	שֵׁנִית
שְׁלִישִׁי	third	שְׁלִישִׁית
רְבִיעִי	fourth	רְבִיעִית
חֲמִישִׁי	fifth	חֲמִישִׁית
שִׁשִּׁי	sixth	שִׁשִּׁית
שְׁבִיעִי	seventh	שְׁבִיעִית
שְׁמִינִי	eighth	שְׁמִינִית
תְּשִׁיעִי	ninth	תְּשִׁיעִית
עֲשִׂירִי	tenth	עֲשִׂירִית

Beginning at eleventh, the cardinal numbers act in place of the ordinals. Ordinals agree or correlate in gender with an accompanying noun:

הַגּוֹרָל הָרִאשׁוֹן 'the first lot' (1 Chron. 24.7)

יוֹם הָאֶחָד וְעֶשְׂרִים 'the twenty-first day' (Exod. 12.18) (observe a permissible absence of the article from יוֹם)

The feminine forms of the ordinal numbers also represent fractions: for example, שְׁלִישִׁית 'one third'. However, certain special terms exist too: namely, חֲצִי 'one half'; שָׁלִישׁ 'one third'; רֹבַע / רֶבַע 'one quarter'; חֹמֶשׁ 'one fifth'; עִשָּׂרוֹן 'one tenth.'

Vocabulary

אֵשׁ	'fire'
בָּנָה	'to build'
דָּם	'blood'
יַעֲקֹב	'Jacob'
יָרַד	'to go down'
לֵוִי	'Levi, Levite'
נְאֻם	'utterance'
נָגַד (הִגִּיד Hiphil)	'to tell'
רוּחַ	'spirit, wind'
שַׁעַר	'gate'

Exercises

1. Underscore the correct demonstrative form in the following phrases/sentences. Then translate them.
   a. בַּיּוֹם < הַהוּא / הַהִיא > (Gen. 15.18)
   b. < אֵלֶּה / הֵמָּה > תוֹלְדוֹת הַשָּׁמַיִם וְהָאָרֶץ (Gen. 2.4)
   c. < הוּא / הִיא > הָעִיר הַגְּדֹלָה (Gen. 10.12)
   d. הָעִיר < הַזֶּה / הַזֹּאת > קְרֹבָה (Gen. 19.20)
   e. הַמַּרְאֶה הַגָּדֹל < הַזֹּאת / הַזֶּה > (Exod. 3.3)

2. Give the English equivalent for these five numerals.
   a. שִׁבְעַת אֲלָפִים
   b. אַרְבָּעִים
   c. אַרְבָּעָה עָשָׂר אֶלֶף
   d. שְׁמֹנָה עָשָׂר וּשְׁלֹשׁ מֵאוֹת
   e. שְׁלֹשִׁים וְשָׁלֹשׁ

LESSON 13

Pronouns (Independent, Suffixed, Relative)

13.1. Independent Pronouns

Independent personal pronouns are written as separate words and are used as subjective pronouns, but not as objective or possessive pronouns. (Special pronominal suffixes—introduced later on in this lesson and in Lesson 19—must be added to nouns, prepositions and verbs to indicate objective and possessive relationships.)

The independent pronouns appear primarily in these forms:

		Singular	Plural
first person	common	אָנֹכִי / אֲנִי 'I' (1cs)	אֲנַחְנוּ 'we' (1cp)
second person	masculine	אַתָּה 'you' (2ms)	אַתֶּם 'you' (2mp)
	feminine	אַתְּ* 'you' (2fs)	אַתֵּן / אַתֵּנָה 'you' (2fp)
third person	masculine	הוּא 'he, it' (3ms)	הֵם / הֵמָּה 'they' (3mp)
	feminine	הִיא 'she, it' (3fs)	הֵנָּה 'they' (3fp)

[*This is one of the few cases where a terminal vowelless letter has a silent šᵉwâ.]

Principally sentences which are nonverbal employ independent pronouns as subjects,* with the linking verb understood (compare Lessons 7.5 and 10.3):

אֲנִי יוֹסֵף   'I am Joseph' (Gen. 45.3)

רְחוֹקָה־הִיא מִצִּידוֹן   'it was far from Sidon' (Judg. 18.28)

[*In verbal sentences pronominal subjects are inherent in the verb forms themselves (see the next lesson, especially Lesson 14.4), so that independent pronouns need not be written. Whenever they are written, it is for the sake of clarity or emphasis.]

A nonverbal sentence can insert a third-person pronoun to serve as a copula:

שְׁלֹשֶׁת הַשָּׂרִגִים שְׁלֹשֶׁת יָמִים הֵם   'the three branches are three days'
(Gen. 40.12)

אַתָּה־הוּא הָאֱלֹהִים   'you are God' (2 Sam. 7.28)

13.2. Suffixed Pronouns on Nouns

When attached directly to nouns, pronominal suffixes function to show possession.

Pronominal suffixes for *singular* nouns are generally the following:

יָ (1cs)	ךָ (2ms)	ךְ (2fs)	וֹ (3ms)	הָ (3fs)*
נוּ (1cp)	כֶם (2mp)	כֶן (2fp)	ם (3mp)	ן (3fp)

[*The mappîq indicates that the He has the full status of an ordinary consonant (recall section 5.2).]

When a noun ends with a guttural consonant, the connecting vowel of 2ms, 2mp and 2fp switches from the simple š⁽e⁾wâ to the composite ḥāṭēp pataḥ.

The shape of the singular noun which receives a suffixed pronoun is rather similar to the construct state, although not infrequently with somwhat different vocalization: for example, שִׁירוֹ 'his/its song'; נְבִיאֲכֶם 'your prophet'; אַדְמָתָהּ 'her/its land'.

Occasionally the final letter of a noun is doubled before a suffix: for example, אִמִּי 'my mother'.

Irregular terms must be learned as encountered: for example, פִּיךָ, 'your mouth', from פֶּה.

Pronominal suffixes for *plural* nouns are generally the following:

יַ (1cs)	יךָ (2ms)*	יִךְ (2fs)	יו (3ms)	יהָ (3fs)*
ינוּ (1cp)	יכֶם (2mp)	יכֶן (2fp)	יהֶם (3mp)	יהֶן (3fp)

[*Treat s⁽e⁾gōl yōd as if it were s⁽e⁾gōl or ṣērê or ṣērê yōd.]

Every suffix of the plural noun contains a yōd; 1cs (יַ) is the only suffix of the singular noun to possess this letter

Dual nouns and masculine plural nouns drop their endings before suffixed pronouns, while feminine plural nouns retain their endings. Vowel alteration may take place in the remaining form: יָדֶיךָ 'your hands'; אַנְשֵׁיהֶן 'their husbands'; בְּנוֹתֵינוּ 'our daughters'.

A noun with a pronominal suffix will always be treated as definite. (See Lesson 11.2 for the other indicators of definiteness.) Therefore a modifying adjective will have the definite article:

מַחֲמַדֵּי הַטֹּבִים   'my good treasures' (Joel 4.5)

13.3. *Suffixed Pronouns on Prepositions*

When joined to the end of prepositions, suffixed pronouns function as objects of those prepositions. Certain prepositions bear pronominal suffixes like those found on singular nouns. However, the connecting vowel generally becomes qāmeṣ gādôl in 2fs, 1cp, 2mp and 2fp. Entirely new forms—הֶם , and הֶן ,—usually substitute for 3mp and 3fp. For example: עִמּוֹ 'with him/it' (incorporating dagesh forte); לָהֶן 'to them'; בָּךְ 'in you'; אִתִּי 'with me', but אִתְּכֶם 'with you' and אִתָּם 'with them'. (Even the definite direct object marker assumes equivalent pronominal suffixes: for example, אוֹתָנוּ, 'us'. Keep in mind that a suffixed את which is pointed with ḥōlem waw or ḥōlem is the object marker, with ḥireq the preposition.)

The prepositions כְּ and מִן are quite irregular.

כָּמוֹנִי (1cs)	כָּמוֹךָ (2ms)	כָּמוֹהוּ (3ms)	כָּמוֹהָ (3fs)
כָּמוֹנוּ (1cp)	כָּכֶם (2mp)	כָּהֶם (3mp)	כָּהֵנָּה (3fp)

מִמֶּנִּי (1cs)	מִמְּךָ (2ms)	מִמֵּךְ (2fs)	מִמֶּנּוּ (3ms)	מִמֶּנָּה (3fs)
מִמֶּנּוּ (1cp)	מִכֶּם (2mp)		מֵהֶם (3mp)	מֵהֵנָּה (3fp)

Certain prepositions use the pronominal suffixes found on plural nouns. Vowel changes may occur in the preposition. For example: עֲלֵיכֶן 'upon you'; אֲלֵיהֶן 'toward them'; אַחֲרֶיךָ 'after you'; תַּחְתֵּינוּ 'under us'; לְפָנָיו 'before him/it'.

It should also be noted that בֵּין mixes suffixes:

בֵּינִי (1cs)	בֵּינְךָ (2ms)	בֵּינֵךְ (2fs)	בֵּינוֹ (3ms)
בֵּינֵינוּ (1cp)	בֵּינֵיכֶם (2mp)	בֵּינֵיהֶם (3mp)	

13.4. *Relative Pronoun*

The relative pronoun אֲשֶׁר—'who, which, that'—normally intervenes between a noun and its qualifying prepositional phrase. Examples help to illustrate:

אִישׁ אֲשֶׁר כָּמֹנִי	'a man (who is) like me' (Gen. 44.15)
הַמַּיִם אֲשֶׁר מִתַּחַת לָרָקִיעַ	'the waters (that were) under the firmament' (Gen. 1.7)

Likewise אֲשֶׁר often links a qualifying verbal clause to its nominal antecedent.*

הָאֲדָמָה אֲשֶׁר פָּצְתָה אֶת־פִּיהָ	'the ground that opened its mouth' (Gen. 4.11)

When the relative pronoun depicts an object, a resumptive or retro-spective pronoun commonly appears. Thus, the Hebrew counterpart of English 'I am Joseph your brother, whom you sold' is אֲשֶׁר־מְכַרְתֶּם אֹתִי אֲנִי יוֹסֵף אֲחִיכֶם (Gen. 45.4), literally, 'I am Joseph your brother, who you sold me'. When the relative pronoun depicts possession, a resump-tive or retrospective pronoun routinely appears. Thus, the Hebrew counterpart of English 'a people whose language you will not under-stand' is גּוֹי אֲשֶׁר לֹא־תִשְׁמַע לְשֹׁנוֹ (Deut. 28.49), literally, 'a people which you will not understand its language'.

[*These samples with verbs will hopefully whet your appetite for next lesson and beyond.]

Vocabulary

אֹהֶל	'tent'
אַהֲרוֹן	'Aaron'
בָּרַךְ	'to bless'
יָרֵא	'to fear'
כְּלִי	'vessel'
מָלַךְ	'to reign'
עָנָה	'to answer'
עֵץ	'tree, wood'
רַע	'bad'
שָׂדֶה	'field'

Exercises

In Judg. 14.1-4 you will discover the words below. Specify which are independent pronouns and which carry suffixed pronouns. Identify the pronominal person, gender and number—use a lexicon if necessary. Finally, provide a translation of each word. (For instance, פָּנָיו carries a suffixed pronoun, third masculine singular, and means 'his/its face'.)

אָבִיו (Hint: waw would be ḥōlem waw were it not pre-ceded by a vowel.)

אוֹתָהּ	אָחִיךְ
אִמּוֹ	אַתָּה
הוּא	הִיא
לוֹ	לִי
עַמִּי	

LESSON 14

Verbs, Qal Perfect

14.1. *Verbs*

Biblical Hebrew verbs have two full inflections for person, gender and number. Sufformatives (or suffixes) on a relatively fixed base mark the first inflection, called 'perfect'. Both preformatives (or prefixes) and sufformatives on a relatively fixed but different base mark the second inflection, called 'imperfect'. They derive their names from the fact that verbs in Semitic languages tend to signify less time of action (past, present, future) than kind of action (complete, incomplete).* The perfect tense represents complete action; the imperfect tense represents incomplete action.

[*Although this is the majority opinion about the signification of verbs, a distinct minority of scholars maintain the opposite view.]

14.2. *Qal Perfect*

We shall start our study of the Hebrew verb with the perfect. The majority of strong verbs in the simple active stem, known as 'Qal', inflect according to this pattern.*

3ms	קָטַל	3cp	קָטְלוּ
3fs	קָטְלָה		
2ms	קָטַלְתָּ	2mp	קְטַלְתֶּם
2fs	קָטַלְתְּ	2fp	קְטַלְתֶּן
1cs	קָטַלְתִּי	1cp	קָטַלְנוּ

[*Lessons 21 to 24 will deal with nonsimple and nonactive stems; from Lesson 25 onwards weak verbs containing phonological peculiarities will be discussed.]

The Qal perfect 3ms form of every strong verb and most weak verbs is disyllabic, possessing three (root) consonants accompanied by two vowels. (It is this base form under which lexicons list those verbs.)

Pronominal elements are appended to this base form to designate the other persons, genders and numbers (see foregoing chart):

הָ 'she'   תָ 'you'   תְ 'you' (silent šᵉwâ)   תִי 'I'

וּ 'they'   תֶם 'you'   תֶן 'you'   נוּ 'we'

These sufformatives are standard for nearly all verbs, whether strong or weak, in all stems.

It should be noted that when a verb's final root consonant is the same as what begins a sufformative, only one letter is written—but with dagesh forte: for example, כָּרַת + תִי produces כָּרַֿתִּי.

The verbal paradigm above reveals how certain sufformatives effect changes in the base form's vocalization as well as accentuation. The 3fs (הָ) and 3cp (וּ) endings cause the pataḥ to reduce to a mobile šᵉwâ. The 2mp (תֶם) and 2fp (תֶן) endings cause the qāmeṣ to reduce to a mobile šᵉwâ. All four of these pronominal components draw the tone/stress to themselves and away from its original position.

Note that a silent šᵉwâ is inserted before every sufformative except those of the third person. This means that the second/final syllable of Qal perfect 2fs verbs terminates with two consonants both of which carry syllable dividers!

Besides the type of verb treated already is a much smaller class with ṣērê or ḥōlem—instead of pataḥ—in the second syllable of Qal perfect third masculine singular. The ṣērê-class inflects otherwise like the pataḥ-class above; the ḥōlem-type does not:

3ms	קָטֹן	3cp	קָטְנוּ
3fs	קָטְנָה		
2ms	קָטֹנְתָ	2mp	קְטָנְתֶם
2fs	קָטֹנְתְ	2fp	קְטָנְתֶן
1cs	קָטֹנְתִי	1cp	קָטֹנוּ

During the early history of the Hebrew language this category of verbs denoted states of being or attributes (for example, מָלֵא 'to be full') rather than action or motion. However, by the stage of Biblical Hebrew some verbs in this category had come to denote action (for example, נָבֵל 'to wither').

14.3. *Verbs and Syntax*

A verb will generally but not always agree in person, gender, and number with its subject. (Observe that the third plural gender is common; so too the first singular and plural.) Two examples from the Hebrew Bible illustrate:

נָתַן הָאֱלֹהִים בְּיָדוֹ אֶת־מִדְיָן   'God gave Midian into his hand' (Judg. 7.14)

אָמַר נָבָל   'a fool said' (Ps. 53.2)

Although the foregoing examples illustrate how verbs commonly precede their subjects, the reverse is also common:

יְהוָה אֱלֹהֵינוּ כָּרַת עִמָּנוּ בְּרִית   'Yahweh our God made a covenant with us' (Deut. 5.2)

The switch in word order can signal emphasis or contrast.

The perfect tense is negated by the particle לֹא, 'not', placed immediately before the verb:

לֹא־שָׁמְרוּ אֲבוֹתֵינוּ אֶת־דְּבַר יְהוָה   'our ancestors did not keep Yahweh's word' (2 Chron. 34.21)

14.4. *Summary*

For now render the perfect tense in one of two ways.*

1. Action verbs most often in past time.

   לֹא צָחַקְתִּי   'I did not laugh' (Gen. 18.15)
   וְרָחֵל לָקְחָה אֶת־הַתְּרָפִים   'and Rachel had taken the idols' (Gen. 31.34)

2. Stative verbs—and others representing perception or disposition—most often in present time:

   אַתָּה זָקַנְתָּ   'you are old' (1 Sam. 8.5)
   אָהַבְתִּי אֶתְכֶם   'I love you' (Mal. 1.2)

[*Lesson 20 in particular will introduce further options.]

Vocabulary

אוֹ	'or'
לֶחֶם	'bread, food'
מִלְחָמָה	'war, battle'
מִשְׁפָּחָה	'clan'
נָבִיא	'prophet'
סָבִיב	'around'

סוּר	'to turn aside'
עָבַד	'to serve'
פָּקַד	'to appoint; visit'
רָעָה	'wickedness'

Exercises

1. Write the full inflection of the Qal perfect (just like the pattern/ paradigm at the outset of this lesson) for זָכַר. Do the same, with appropriate adjustments, for חָפֵץ and שָׁכֹל.

2. For each of the following state: (1) its person, gender and number; (2) its dictionary—that is 3ms—form; and (3) its English translation.

    a.   נָפְלָה

    b.   לְקַחְתֶּם

    c.   אָהַבְתָּ

    d.   שָׁמַעְנוּ

    e.   עָבַדְתִּי

LESSON 15

Qal Imperfect

15.1. Action Verbs

In Lesson 14.1 it was implied that the imperfect inflection is chiefly a conjugation with preformatives, although sufformatives are also present. It has also been stated that the imperfect tense putatively connotes an incomplete action.

The main inflectional pattern for strong verbs in Qal imperfect appears thus:

3ms	יִקְטֹל	3mp	יִקְטְלוּ
3fs	תִּקְטֹל	3fp	תִּקְטֹלְנָה
2ms	תִּקְטֹל	2mp	תִּקְטְלוּ
2fs	תִּקְטְלִי	2fp	תִּקְטֹלְנָה
1cs	אֶקְטֹל	1cp	נִקְטֹל

Since the 3fs and 2ms are formally identical, context will have to determine a distinction. The same is true for the 3fp and 2fp.

The singular preformatives are yōd, three taws and aleph. The plural preformatives are yōd, three taws, and nun. To put it another way, aleph is used for singular and nun for plural in the first person; yōd is used for both singular and plural masculine in the third person; while taw is employed for all else. Every preformative takes a ḥireq vowel, except for aleph which takes sᵉgōl.

Among the imperfect singular verbs the sole sufformative found is ḥireq yōd on the second feminine. The first four forms of the plural have sufformatives alternating between šûreq (masculine) and nun + qāmeṣ + he (feminine). Only the first person lacks a sufformative on the plural.

Hence, the chart of pronominal elements attaching to the imperfect's hypothetical base form קְטֹל is*

ַ__יְ	__תְ	__תְ	ְ_ַ_תְ	__אֶ
'he'	'she'	'you'	'you'	'I'

וּ__יְ	נָה__תְ	וּ__תְ	נָה__תְ	__נְ
'they'	'they'	'you'	'you'	'we'

[*A variant ending וּן (rather than וּ) on 3mp and 2mp verbs is encountered with relative frequency: for example, תִּקְרְבוּן; On a few occasions יִן replaces ְ_ַ on 2fs: for example, תִּדְבָּקִין (on this occasion in pause).]

Like the perfect inflection, the imperfect sufformatives can cause alteration of vowels and accents. The 2fs, 3mp and 2mp endings (ְ_ַ and וּ) draw the tone to themselves and produce a reduction from an original ḥōlem to a substitute mobile šᵉwâ. A syllable divider must be placed under a verb's third root letter when it is succeeded by the 3fp and 2fp sufformative (נָה). Incidentally, the šᵉwâ beneath the initial root consonant is silent and closes the syllable containing the preformative.

15.2. *Stative Forms*
Stative verbs consistently replace the ḥōlem with a pataḥ in the Qal imperfect:

למד

3ms	יִלְמַד	3mp	יִלְמְדוּ
3fs	תִּלְמַד	3fp	תִּלְמַדְנָה
2ms	תִּלְמַד	2mp	תִּלְמְדוּ
2fs	תִּלְמְדִי	2fp	תִּלְמַדְנָה
1cs	אֶלְמַד	1cp	נִלְמַד

שכל

3ms	יִשְׂכַּל	3mp	יִשְׂכְּלוּ
3fs	תִּשְׂכַּל	3fp	תִּשְׂכַּלְנָה
2ms	תִּשְׂכַּל	2mp	תִּשְׂכְּלוּ
2fs	תִּשְׂכְּלִי	2fp	תִּשְׂכַּלְנָה
1cs	אֶשְׂכַּל	1cp	נִשְׂכַּל

15.3. *Summary*
Even though the imperfect tense may convey a variety of senses, for the time being render it either:

1. Future:

     תִּמְלֹךְ עַל־יִשְׂרָאֵל   'you will reign over Israel' (1 Sam. 23.17) or

2. Present:

יִדְרְכוּ כֹהֲנֵי דָגוֹן   'the priests of Dagon walk' (1 Sam. 5.5).

Negation of the imperfect matches that of the perfect—through לֹא:

לוֹא־אֶפְקֹד   'I will not punish' (Jer. 5.9).

Vocabulary

בָּבֶל	'Babylon'
חָזַק*	'to be(come) strong'
חַטָּאת	'sin'
חָיָה	'to live'
כָּרַת	'to cut'
מְאֹד	'very'
עֹלָה	'burnt offering'
עֵת	'time'
קָרַב*	'to draw near'
שְׁלֹמֹה	'Solomon'

[*We would expect חָזֵק and קָרֵב as third masculine singular in the perfect, but the pataḥ of action verbs has ousted the ṣērê of stative verbs.]

Exercises

1. Write the Qal imperfect paradigm for the verb whose lexical (or dictionary) form is שָׁמַר (hint: the hypothetical base is שְׁמֹר). Do the same for כָּבֵד.

2. Record (1) the tense (that is perfect or imperfect); (2) the person, gender and number; (3) the root or lexicographic entry (that is Qal perfect 3ms); and (4) the English equivalent of the following verb forms.
    a. נָפְלוּ
    b. יִלְמְדוּן
    c. אֶשְׁבּוֹר
    d. אָמַרְתִּי
    e. תִּזְכְּרִי
    f. תִּגְנֹב
    g. פָּקַד
    h. נִשְׂרֹף

LESSON 16

Volitives in Qal (Cohortative, Imperative, Jussive)

16.1. The Cohortative

An extension of the imperfect in the first person to express emphasis or effort is called cohortative. It is marked by a sufformative הָ appended onto the imperfect. This sufformative draws the accent to itself, causing reduction of the preceding vowel to šᵉwâ.

The cohortative indicates the desire, intention, or determination of a speaker or speakers. The entreating particle נָא ('please' or 'I/we pray' or left untranslated) occurs very often after a cohortative—in which case the nun receives a euphonic dagesh (see Lesson 4.4).

אֶשְׁמְרָה תוֹרָתֶךָ   'I *will* keep your law' (Ps. 119.44) (emphasis)

נִכְרְתָה בְרִית   'Let us make a covenant' (Gen. 31.44)

אֶעְבְּרָה־נָּא   'Let me pass, I pray' (Judg. 11.17)

Note that the normal imperfect form can also be used with a cohortative nuance: נִכְרָת־בְּרִית 'Let us make a covenant' (Ezra 10.3) (qāmeṣ qāṭān for ḥōlem in a closed unaccented syllable).

16.2. The Imperative

The imperative inflects on the analogy of the second person imperfect but leaves off the preformatives. The first of the two šᵉwâs then remaining at the beginning of the 2fs and 2mp turns into a ḥireq (compare Lesson 8.1).

	Action verb		Stative verb
ms	שְׁפֹט*	ms	שְׁכַב*
fs	שִׁפְטִי	fs	שִׁכְבִי
mp	שִׁפְטוּ	mp	שִׁכְבוּ
fp	שְׁפֹטְנָה	fp	שְׁכַבְנָה

[*A sufformative הָ appears frequently on the masculine singular imperative with no striking modification of meaning: for example, action verb שָׁפְטָה (observe qāmeṣ Qāṭān rather than ḥireq in the initial syllable); stative verb שִׁכְבָה.]

Imperatives are used to denote only positive, not negative, commands. (See Lesson 16.3 on the jussive.) The particle נָא may follow any imperative:

שְׁמַע יִשְׂרָאֵל	'Listen, O Israel' (Deut. 5.1)
שִׁמְעִי דְּבַר־יְהוָה	'Hear the word of Yahweh' (Ezek. 16.35)
שִׁפְטוּ־נָא	'Please judge' (Isa. 5.3)

16.3. *The Jussive*

The jussive involves third person imperfect forms.* In strong verbs, Qal jussive takes the same shape as Qal imperfect and therefore must be identified from the context.

[*Quite seldom, first-person or second-person forms are attested. The special case for prohibitions is discussed below.]

A jussive expresses the desire, wish, or command of a speaker or speakers where a different person or group of people is the subject of the verb. The particle נָא is sometimes added behind jussives:

יִשְׁפֹּט יְהוָה	'May Yahweh judge' (1 Sam. 24.13)
יִזְכָּר־נָא הַמֶּלֶךְ	'Let the king recall, I pray' (2 Sam. 14.11)
	(again qāmeṣ qāṭān)

Hebrew conveys second-person prohibitions by means of either the adverb אַל + a jussive verb or the adverb לֹא + an imperfect verb. The former (which can be accompanied by נָא) seems to indicate an immediate, specific prohibition: for example, אַל־תִּשְׁכָּחִי 'Do not forget' (Ps. 103.2), that is, 'Do not now forget'. The latter seems to indicate a permanent, absolute prohibition—like those found in the Decalogue: for example, לֹא תִגְנֹב 'You shall not steal' (Exod. 20.15), that is, 'Never steal'.

Vocabulary

אֶבֶן	'stone'
אֹיֵב	'enemy'
אַף	'nose; anger'
בְּרִית	'covenant'
בָּשָׂר	'flesh'
חֹדֶשׁ	'month, new moon'
מִדְבָּר	'wilderness'

פְּלִשְׁתִּי   'Philistine'

פַּרְעֹה   'Pharaoh'

צֹאן   'flock (of sheep or goats)'

Exercises

Translate these volitives:

a. קִבְרוּ אֹתִי (Gen. 49.29)
b. לֹא תִּגְנֹבוּ (a pausal form for תִּגְנְבוּ, Lev. 19.11)
c. אַל־תִּזְכְּרוּ (Isa. 43.18)
d. שִׁכְבִי עִמִּי (2 Sam. 13.11)
e. שְׁמַע־נָא (Job 42.4)
f. כְּתֹב עָלֶיהָ (Jer. 36.28)
g. אֶשְׁמְרָה דְרָכַי (Ps. 39.2)
h. שִׁמְעָה עַמִּי (Ps. 50.7)
i. נִשְׁלְחָה אֲנָשִׁים (Deut. 1.22)

LESSON 17

Qal Infinitives (Construct, Absolute)

17.1. *Infinitives*

Infinitives are verbal nouns, having both nominal and verbal functions: compare English 'to go' or 'to see'. As verbs, infinitives are infinite in the sense that they express the basic notion of a root without the limitations of gender, number or person. (Perfects, imperfects and volitives— finite verbs—hold such limitations.) As nouns, infinitives sometimes behave like English gerunds, which words typically terminate with *ing* on the order of 'believing' or 'speaking'. Biblical Hebrew has two kinds of infinitive: namely, infinitive construct and infinitive absolute.

17.2. *The Construct*

Among strong verbs the infinitive construct of an action verb is identical in form to the masculine singular imperative: for example, קְטֹל. This is seldom the situation for stative verbs, whose vowels ordinarily imitate those of action verbs: for example, שְׁאוֹל (not שְׁאַל) but שְׁכַב.

Infinitive constructs may be employed without prepositions:

הִנֵּה שְׁמֹעַ מִזֶּבַח טוֹב   'Behold, to obey is better than sacrifice'
(1 Sam. 15.22).

However, the most frequent use of the infinitive construct is with prepositions—especially בְּ, כְּ and לְ.*

[*When a term's second radical (or root letter) is a Begadkefat, it usually remains fricative or soft after בְּ and כְּ but becomes plosive or hard after לְ: for example, לִנְפֹּל, כִּנְפֹל, בִּנְפֹל.]

An infinitive construct + either בְּ or כְּ will most often express a temporal clause:

בִּנְפֹל תַּרְדֵּמָה עַל־אֲנָשִׁים   'while stupor has fallen upon people'
(Job 4.13) (literally, 'in the having
fallen of stupor upon people')

כִּשְׁכַב אֲדֹנִי־הַמֶּלֶךְ עִם־אֲבֹתָיו   'when my lord the king lies down with
his ancestors' (1 Kgs 1.21) (literally,
'as the lying down of my lord the king
with his ancestors')

An infinitive construct + לְ can be used to express a wide variety of
senses, often connoting purpose or result:

תִּשְׁמַע בְּקוֹל יהוה אֱלֹהֶיךָ   'You shall obey Yahweh your God by
לִשְׁמֹר מִצְוֹתָיו וְחֻקֹּתָיו   observing his commandments and
decrees' (Deut. 30.10) (literally, 'you
shall hear "in" the voice of Yahweh
your God to observe his commandments and his decrees')

עֵת לִדְרוֹשׁ אֶת־יהוה   'It is time to seek Yahweh' (Hos.
10.12) (literally, 'time (is) to seek
Yahweh'; notice how English translation requires the insertion of the im-
personal subject *it*)

The infinitive construct is negated by לְבִלְתִּי.

לְבִלְתִּי שְׂרֹף אֶת־הַמְּגִלָּה   'not to burn the scroll' (Jer. 36.25)
לְבִלְתִּי שְׁמֹר מִצְוֹתָיו   'not to keep his commandments'
(Deut. 8.11)

17.3. *The Absolute*

The infinitive absolute of strong verbs—either action or stative—
assumes a qāmeṣ (gādôl) in its first syllable and a ḥōlem waw or ḥōlem
in its second: for example, לָמֹד ,קָטוֹל. Unlike the construct, the absolute
is governed by a preposition only abnormally.

Sometimes infinitive absolutes are used substantively, in a gerundial
manner:

*הִנֵּה שָׂשׂוֹן וְשִׂמְחָה הָרֹג בָּקָר   'There was joy and festivity, killing
וְשָׁחֹט צֹאן   oxen and slaughtering sheep' (Isa.
22.13)

[*Despite appearances שָׂשׂוֹן is not an infinitive but a plain noun.]

More commonly an infinitive absolute acts adverbially, particularly whenever it stands before or behind a finite verb from the same root.

1. When the infinitive precedes, it tends to signify emphasis:

אֱלֹהִים פָּקֹד יִפְקֹד   'God will surely visit you' (Gen. 50.24)
אֶתְכֶם   (literally, 'God to visit will visit you')

2. When the infinitive follows, it tends to signify duration.

לַשָּׁוְא צָרַף צָרוֹף   'In vain he continued refining' (Jer. 6.29) (literally, 'In vain he refined to refine')

An infinitive absolute can substitute for a finite verb, especially an imperative:

זָכוֹר אֶת־הַיּוֹם הַזֶּה   'Remember this day' (Exod. 13.3)
בָּטוֹחַ עַל־תֹּהוּ   'They rely on emptiness'(Isa. 59.4)

Vocabulary

אַמָּה	'cubit'
גְּבוּל	'border'
חַיִל	'strength, army'
חֶסֶד	'kindness'
מַטֶּה	'rod; tribe'
מָלֵא	'to be full'
נַעַר	'lad'
רֶגֶל	'foot'
רָשָׁע	'guilty'
שָׁלוֹם	'peace'

Exercises

Parse and translate the words pointed out below. Parsing/analyzing means to state the stem, tense, person, gender, number and root of a verb. Every sample here will be Qal since the other stems have not yet been encountered. Perfect, imperfect, cohortative, imperative, jussive, infinitive construct, and infinitive absolute all count as tenses. Remember that infinitives do not have person, gender or number. The term 'root' is the three consonants under which dictionaries list verbs.

    a. Deut. 5.12: first word
    b. Isa. 40.2: second word which has a qāmeṣ under its initial consonant

c. Isa. 40.4: term with 'atnāḥ*
d. Ezek. 37.3: word with sillûq*
e. Ezek. 37.5: second term
f. Ps. 1.1: term with sillûq*
g. Ps. 2.1: second word
h. Ps. 2.6: second word
i. Ps. 2.8: first term
j. Ps. 2.11: first word

[*qāmeṣ gādôl replaced šᵉwâ or pataḥ because of pause (section 3.2).]

LESSON 18

Qal Participles

18.1. Defining the Participle

Participles may be regarded as verbal adjectives. They do not reflect person but do reflect both number and gender. They can be either singular or plural and either masculine or feminine. Participial inflection also indicates either an active voice—like English 'making' or 'writing'—or passive voice—like English 'redeemed' or 'sought'—in the Qal stem. None of the other stems (discussed later in Lessons 21–24) have participles with both voices.

18.2. The Form of the Participle

The masculine singular active participle is pointed with a ḥōlem (or ḥōlem waw) in the first syllable and a ṣērê in the second: for example, קֹטֵל / קוֹטֵל. To this form the feminine singular mostly appends a sᵉgōl + taw but sometimes qāmeṣ + he: for example, קֹטֶלֶת / קוֹטְלָה. (Note the accent and vowel changes.) The masculine plural and feminine plural add their respective endings, ḥireq yōd + mem and ḥōlem waw (or ḥōlem) + taw: for example, קוֹטְלֹת, קֹטְלִים.*

[*Many stative verbs substitute a form which in this grammar we will regard as an ordinary adjective rather than listing it as a participle: for example, כָּבֵד, כְּבֵדָה, שְׁלֵלוֹת, שְׁלֵלִים, שָׁלֵל and כְּבֵדוֹת, כְּבֵדִים.]

The masculine singular passive participle is pointed with a qāmeṣ in the first syllable and a šûreq (or qibbûṣ) in the second: for example, קָטוּל. The feminine singular always ends in qāmeṣ + he; the plurals terminate as expected (all three produce vowel reduction): for example, קְטוּלָה, קְטוּלוֹת, קְטֻלִים.

18.3. The Function of the Participle

Biblical Hebrew participles function principally as (1) predicates, (2) attributes and (3) substantives.

1. Predicate participles agree with their subject nouns or pronouns in gender and number but never take the (definite) article. This class of participle is divisible into a pair of further groupings: that is, predicate participles employed adjectivally and those employed verbally.

   a. Adjectival use. In such instances a participle surfaces where it could be replaced by another adjective rather than by a different part of speech:

   וִיהוֹשֻׁעַ הָיָה לָבֵשׁ   'and Joshua was dressed' (Zech. 3.3) (Some other adjective—like עַז 'strong'—could substitute for the term לָבֵשׁ)

   b. Verbal use. Here a participle acts as the verb in an otherwise verbless clause:

   שְׂרָפִים עֹמְדִים מִמַּעַל לוֹ   'seraphim were standing above (literally, from [the] top [with reference] to) him' (Isa. 6.2)

   שׁוֹרְךָ טָבוּחַ לְעֵינֶיךָ   'your ox will be slaughtered before (literally, to the eyes of) you' (Deut. 28.31)

The foregoing illustrations reveal how active participles describe continuing activity, passive participles culminated activity. The time of a participle can be determined only by the environment in which it stands.

2. When used attributively, participles match the number, gender and definiteness of their corresponding nouns. These Hebrew participles often have the force of English relative clauses:

   אֵשׁ אֹכְלָה הוּא   'he is a consuming fire'(Deut. 4.24)

   אִשָּׁה שֹׁכֶבֶת מַרְגְּלֹתָיו   'a woman (who was) lying at his feet' (Ruth 3.8)

   הָאָלוֹת הַכְּתוּבוֹת עַל־הַסֵּפֶר   'the curses which are written on the scroll' (2 Chron. 34.24)

3. Participles as substantives—that is, nouns—signify the person performing a certain action. They may be indefinite or definite, masculine or feminine, singular or plural, absolute or con-

struct. Participial nouns may be used as subjects, direct objects, appositives, prepositional objects, predicates and so on:

דָּרְשׁוּ הַשֹּׁפְטִים	'the judges inquired' (Deut. 19.18) (definite, masculine, plural, absolute, subject)
הֲשֹׁמֵר אָחִי אָנֹכִי	'am I my brother's keeper?' (Gen. 4.9) (definite, masculine, singular, construct, predicate)

Vocabulary

אַבְרָהָם (אַבְרָם)	'Abraham (Abram)'
אֵל	'God'
זָכַר	'to remember'
זֶרַע	'seed, offspring'
חָטָא	'to sin'
חַי	'alive'
יָרַשׁ	'to inherit'
לַיְלָה	'night'
מַעֲשֶׂה	'work'
עָוֹן	'iniquity'

Exercises

1. Analyze and translate these verbs. (Count 'participle' as a category of *tense*. In the Qal stem alone you must further mark a participle as either active or passive.)

    a. שֹׁמְרֵי
    b. שָׁמְעוּ
    c. עָזַבְתָּ
    d. לִכְתֹּב
    e. אֶזְכֹּר

2. Underline the correct participial form for the following clauses and translate the complete phrase.

    a. הָאִישׁ > הַשֹּׁכֵב / הַשֹּׁכֶבֶת < עִמָּהּ (Deut. 22.29)
    b. > בְּרוּכִים / בְּרוּכוֹת < אַתֶּם לַיהוָה (Ps. 115.15)
    c. הֲלֹא־הִיא > כָּתוּב / כְּתוּבָה < עַל־סֵפֶר הַיָּשָׁר (Jos. 10.13)
    d. אַחֲרֵי מִי אַתָּה > רֹדֵף / רֹדְפָה < (1 Sam. 24.15)
    e. וְיָדַיִם > שֹׁפְכִים / שֹׁפְכוֹת < דָּם־נָקִי (Prov. 6.17)

LESSON 19

Suffixes on Qal Verbs

19.1. Pronominal Suffixes
When the direct object of a verb is a pronoun, the pronominal suffix might be joined to the object marker אֵת (Lesson 13.3) and placed either before or after the verb. Another option is for the object pronoun to be suffixed directly onto the end of the verb. No difference in meaning exists between the two constructions.

The pronominal suffixes attached to a verb are practically the same as those attached to a singular noun (see Lesson 13.2). They appear as follows—minus any linking or connecting vowels:

1cs	נִי*	'me'	1cp	נוּ	'us'
2ms	ךָ	'you'	2mp	כֶם	'you'
2fs	ךְ	'you'	2fp	כֶן	'you'
3ms	הוּ or וֹ	'him'	3mp	ם	'them'
3fs	הָ or הָ	'her'	3fp	ן	'them'

With the exception of the participles, the 2fp suffixed pronoun occurs on no verb in the Masoretic Text.

[*The prepositions כְּ and מִן displayed this suffix.]

19.2. Perfect with Suffixes
The altered Qal perfect forms of action verbs which precede a suffix are:

קְטָל	(3ms)
קְטָלַת	(3fs)*
קְטַלְתָּ	(2ms)
קְטַלְתִּי	(2fs and 1cs)
קְטָלוּ	(3cp)
קְטַלְתּוּ	(2mp and 2fp)
קְטַלְנוּ	(1cp)

[*qāmeṣ (gādôl) will replace pataḥ in advance of the suffixes 2fs and 3mp.]

Whenever a vowel intervenes between one of these verb forms and one of the suffixes above, that vowel will usually be a pataḥ or a qāmeṣ: (without linking vowel inserted) יְדָעְתִּיךְ; (with linking vowel inserted) לְקַחְתָּנוּ, שְׁלָחַנִי.

However, the connecting vowel will be mobile šᵉwâ before 2ms and ṣērê or sᵉgōl before 2fs suffixes; whenever the 3ms suffix is the lone waw, a connecting ḥōlem goes over it!: שְׁפָטוֹ; שְׁלָחֵךְ; נְתָנוּ.

The he of the הוּ and הָ suffixes normally assimilates to the taw of קָטְלַת (Qal perfect 3fs), resulting in forms like קְטָלַתּוּ and קְטָלַתָּה. (Observe how an extra He is tacked onto the end here.) Since Hebrew uses niphal and hithpael stems [Lessons 21 and 24] to express the reflexive voice, Qal perfect 2fs does not take second-person suffixes nor does Qal perfect 1cs does not take first-person suffixes. Fortunately, textual environment will eliminate the possibility of confusion whenever these Qal forms take third-person suffixes. While the choice of suffixed pronouns and connecting vowels is identical for Qal perfect 3ms and 2ms, each has a different shape (קְטָל and קְטַלְתּ respectively) preceding those suffixes.

Characteristic of ḥōlem-class stative verbs with pronominal suffixes will be the appearance of an 'o' vowel (qāmeṣ qāṭān or ḥōlem) in the altered verbal root; characteristic of ṣērê-class verbs will be ṣērê in the third-person forms of the altered root: for example, שְׁכֵחוּךְ, יְכָלְתִּיו.

19.3. *Imperfect and Imperative with Suffixes*
The altered Qal imperfect forms of action verbs which precede a suffix are:

יִקְטְל	(3ms)*
תִּקְטְל	(3fs and 2ms)*
תִּקְטְלִי	(2fs)
אֶקְטְל	(1cs)*
יִקְטְלוּ	(3mp)
תִּקְטְלוּ	(3fp and 2mp and 2fp)
נִקְטְל	(1cp)*

[*Qāmeṣ qāṭān replaces the second šᵉwâ—reading from right to left before the suffixes 2ms and 2mp. Qāmeṣ gādôl appears as the substitute vowel for that šᵉwâ in such forms before *all* pronominal suffixes when the verb is stative, except where the vowel becomes pataḥ ahead of the 2mp suffix: for example, יִלְבָּשֵׁנִי, נִלְבָּשְׁכֶם. (The stative equivalents to the imperfects appearing without asterisk consistently show qāmeṣ [gādôl] instead of a second šᵉwâ: for example, תִּלְבָּשִׁין.)]

Whenever a vowel intervenes between one of these verb forms and one of the suffixes above, that vowel will usually be a ṣērê or a sᵉgōl: (without linking vowel inserted) יְרְדְּפוּנִי; (with linking vowel inserted) יִכְתְּבֵם. However, the connecting vowel will be qāmeṣ when the 3fs suffix is he containing mappîq: for example, יִשְׂרְפָה.

Occasionally a (so-called 'energic') nun intrudes ahead of the 2ms, 3ms and 3fs suffixes. Since assimilation almost always takes place, the shapes of the suffixes with linking vowel appear as ךָ֫ , נּוּ֫ and נָּה֫ — rather than נְךָ֫ , נְהוּ֫ and נְהָ֫ : for example, תִּזְכְּרֶ֫נּוּ.

There is no difference in meaning between a suffix which has the additional nun and one which does not.

The altered Qal imperative forms of action verbs which precede a suffix are:

קְטָל (ms)   קִטְלִי (fs)   קִטְלוּ (mp and fp)

The choice of suffix and connecting vowel—including the ability to attract an energic nun—is in every instance the same for imperatives as for imperfects: for example, עָזְרֵ֫נוּ.

19.4. *The Infinitive Construct with Suffixes*
The altered Qal infinitive construct shape of action verbs which precede a suffix is identical with the imperative masculine singular, namely, קְטָל.*

[*Sometimes we find קְטֹל or even, only before the 2ms and 2mp suffixes, קָטָל or קָטֹל (all qāmeṣ qāṭāns).]

It will be seen that the suffixes and linking vowels employed by the infinitive construct are exactly the same as those employed by singular nouns (Lesson 13.2), except for one alternative (נִי) in the 1cs. You will discover, moreover, that suffixes on an infinitive may denote either its subject or object—again with the exception that the 1cs alternate נִי must represent the object, while י can represent either: for example, זָכְרֵ֫נוּ 'our (act of) remembering' or 'to remember us'; הָרְגֵ֫נִי 'to kill me'; קָרְבְכֶם 'your (act of) approaching' or 'to approach you'.

19.5. *Participle with Suffixes*
Plural Qal participles take suffixes of the plural noun and singular participles usually assume pronominal suffixes of the singular noun (see

Lesson 13.2). Naturally such participles are in construct: שֹׂפְכוֹ ;אֹיְבֵי; שִׂנְאוֹתַיִךְ.

Note that Paradigm 2, 'Strong Verb in Qal with Suffixes', provides a comprehensive display of all the forms just discussed.

Vocabulary

אֲדָמָה	'ground'
אֵם	'mother'
בָּקַשׁ (Piel בִּקֵּשׁ)	'to seek'
יְהוֹשֻׁעַ	'Joshua'
כָּתַב	'to write'
מוֹעֵד	'appointed place or time'
נַחֲלָה	'possession'
קֶרֶב	'midst'
רָבָה	'to be(come) numerous'
תּוֹרָה	'law'

Exercises

1. Turn to the book of Ruth. Locate and copy the suffixed verbs, one each in 1.16, 2.9 and 3.4. Analyze and translate those three verbs. (To the half-dozen parsing categories of verbal root, stem, tense, person, gender and number already encountered, now add the category of 'other features'. There you will include information—gender, number and person—about any pronominal suffix. You should also start recording in that division a mention of any preposition adhering to an infinitive construct.)

2. Do the same for the single suffixed verb in Hag. 1.12 and the two in 2.22.

LESSON 20

Waw Consecutive, Verbal Hendiadys

20.1. *Waw Consecutive after Perfect and Imperfect*
A passage that narrates consecutive events in past time will often begin with a perfect and then continue with a series of imperfects sustaining waw consecutive.

זָכַרְתִּי בַלַּיְלָה שִׁמְךָ יְהוָה וָאֶשְׁמְרָה
תּוֹרָתֶךָ

'I have remembered your name, O Yahweh, at night and have kept your law' (Ps. 119.55)

Smooth English renderings ought in many circumstances to incorporate subordinating arrangements such as adverbial clauses or participial modifiers:

וְהָאָדָם יָדַע אֶת־חַוָּה אִשְׁתּוֹ וַתַּהַר
וַתֵּלֶד אֶת־קָיִן

'After Adam had intercourse with his wife Eve, she conceived and bore Cain' (Gen. 4.1)*

[*Intermittently throughout this lesson nonsimple (that is, non-Qal) stems and non-strong (that is, weak) verbs will be encountered. In the foregoing sentence וַתַּהַר is from a lamedh–he verb הָרָה (See Lesson 33); וַתֵּלֶד is from a pe–yōd/waw verb יָלַד (see Lesson 28).]

A little less frequently—but with a wider range of meanings—an imperfect will start a passage while one or more perfects will conclude it:

בְּיַד־מֶלֶךְ בָּבֶל תִּנָּתֵן וּשְׂרָפָהּ בָּאֵשׁ

'It will be given [Niphal stem of נָתַן, Lesson 21] into the hand of Babylon's king, and he will burn it with fire' (Jer. 21.10)

לְמַעַן תִּזְכְּרִי וָבֹשְׁתְּ

'In order that you may remember and so be ashamed [from Hollow verb בּוֹשׁ; see Lesson 30]' (Ezek. 16.63)

יִשָּׂאוּם הָרָצִים וֶהֱשִׁיבוּם   'The couriers used to carry them [from pe–nun and lamedh–aleph verb נָשָׂא; see Lessons 27 and 32] and return them [Hiphil stem of a hollow verb שׁוּב; see Lessons 23 and 30]' (1 Kgs 14.28)

From these examples it can be seen that the verb that stands first in such a series determines both the time (past or future) and the mood (indicative or subjunctive) of the verbs that come next. In the first two examples of this section both sentences show past time and indicative mood. Of the three examples just given the first sample exhibits future indicative; the second illustration displays present-future time and subjunctive mood; the third instance manifests past indicative along with an aspect of habitual or repeated action.

From the examples provided it is also possible to observe that the waw-consecutive verbs function to signal either temporal sequence/succession or logical consequence/result. It is not always possible to draw a sharp distinction between these two meanings nor is it always necessary to express the distinction in translation.

    The narrative use of perfects and especially imperfects that bore waw consecutive became so commonplace that without a preceding imperfect or perfect they could begin a verse, chapter, or even entire book.

וַיִּתְחַזֵּק שְׁלֹמֹה בֶן־דָּוִיד עַל־מַלְכוּתוֹ   'Now David's son Solomon established himself [Hithpael stem of חָזַק; see Lesson 24] over his realm', at the outset of 2 Chron. 1.1.

20.2. *Waw Consecutive after other Tenses*
An imperative verb may serve as a governing term when it is placed before a perfect, which in this co-ordinate relationship must be translated as an imperative:

שִׁמְעוּ אֶת־דִּבְרֵי הַבְּרִית   'Hear the words of this covenant and
הַזֹּאת וַעֲשִׂיתֶם אוֹתָם   do [from pe–guttural and lamedh–he verb עָשָׂה; see Lessons 25 and 33] them' (Jer. 11.6)

Likewise an infinitive absolute employed with the force of an imperative may come ahead of a perfect with waw consecutive:

שְׁמֹעַ בֵּין־אֲחֵיכֶם וּשְׁפַטְתֶּם צֶדֶק 'Examine your compatriots and
judge righteously'(Deut. 1.16)

Finally, a participle which describes an impending action may appear in
advance of a waw-consecutive perfect. (In particular, participles introduced by הִנֵּה might refer to something destined to take place in the near
future.)

הִנְּךָ הוֹלֵךְ מֵאִתִּי וְהִכְּךָ הָאַרְיֵה 'As soon as you walk away from me,
a lion will kill you [Hiphil stem of a
pronominally suffixed pe–nun and
lamedh–he verb נָכָה; see Lessons 23,
27 and 33]' (1 Kgs 20.36)*

[*Here הִנֵּה accepts the second masculine singular pronoun.]

This final example points out how the subject need not be the same in
every clause of a sequence.

20.3. *Morphology of Waw Consecutives*
The waw consecutive which attaches to the perfect tense is vocalized
like the waw conjunction according to the regular rules given in Lesson
7.3. The third, fourth and fifth examples given in section 1 of the present lesson demonstrate this.

The waw consecutive which adheres to the imperfect is written waw
+ pataḥ + dagesh forte in the following root letter. (The aleph preformative of the first common singular, however, rejects the dagesh and
causes substitution of a qāmeṣ for the pataḥ.) The first two examples
given in the first section of this lesson represent these traits.

The consecutive perfect tends to move the tone to the last syllable in
the first common singular and second masculine singular but not in the
first common plural: שָׁפַטְתִּי becoming וְשָׁפַטְתִּי; לָקַחְתָּ becoming וְלָקַחְתָּ.

The consecutive imperfect favours shifting the stress away from the
final syllable. This change presents itself only with certain weak verbs:
תְּגָרֵשׁ becoming וַתְּגָרֶשׁ (Piel stem of an ayin–guttural verb גָּרַשׁ; see Lessons 22 and 29).

This last illustration shows how an imperfect can alter its punctuation
when combined with the consecutive waw. Besides vowel change, consonant elimination may also be witnessed. Again certain weak verbs

experience this change: יִגְלֶה becoming וַיִּגֶל (from lamedh-he verb גָּלָה; see Lesson 33).

A contrasting tendency surfaces in the secondary 1cs form וָאֶקְטְלָה, which is longer than the normal form וָאֶקְטֹל. (The הָ possesses no semantic value.)

20.4. *Verbal Hendiadys*

A number of Hebrew verbs may be juxtaposed in front of another verb, with or without a waw present. Rather than acting as a fully independent, the first term serves to qualify the second. Those anterior terms most commonly used in this way are:

In the Qal stem	In the Hiphil stem	In the Piel stem
שׁוּב (hollow)	יָסַף (pe–yōd/waw)	מהר (ayin–guttural)**
קוּם (hollow)	יאל (pe–yōd/waw)**	
הָלַךְ*	שכם**	
	רָבָה (lamedh–he)	

[*הָלַךְ behaves along the lines of pe–yōd/waws.
**Since forms of מְהַר, יאל and שְׁכַם are in reality altogether absent from Qal, it is appropriate here to omit the vowel points from these roots.]

Consult a lexicon under each verb for details about its idiom. Examples from the Hebrew Bible will help to clarify:

Examples:

קוּם־נָא שְׁבָה 'Come on (and) sit' (literally, 'Arise [and] sit') (Gen. 27.19)

וַיְמַהֲרוּ וַיַּשְׁכִּימוּ וַיֵּצְאוּ 'And they went forth quickly early in the morning' (literally, 'And they hurried and they got up early and they went out' Here a pair of supplementary verbs precede the main verb) (Josh. 8.14).

הוֹאִיל הָלַךְ 'He has willingly gone' (literally, 'He has resolved and he has gone') (Hos. 5.11)

Vocabulary

אָהֵב	'to love'	
בֶּגֶד	'garment'	
יוֹסֵף	'Joseph'	
יָסַף	'to add'	

כּוּן (Niphal נָכוֹן)   'to be firm or established'

מַחֲנֶה   'camp'

מַלְאָךְ   'messenger, angel'

מִנְחָה   'gift, offering'

נָצַל (Hiphil הִצִּיל)   'to deliver'

שָׁתָה   'to drink'

Exercises

Translate the five sentences. (All but the last sample represent an abridged form of the scriptural text.) For example:

הַיָּם הוֹלֵךְ וְסֹעֵר עֲלֵיהֶם וַיִּקְרְאוּ אֶל־יְהוָה 'The sea went on growing stormy against them, and they called unto Yahweh' (Jon. 1.13-14)

a. בָּא נְבוּזַרְאֲדָן וַיִּשְׂרֹף אֶת־בֵּית־יְהוָה (2 Kgs 25.8-9; בָּא is Qal perfect 3ms from בּוֹא, the dictionary form)

b. שָׁמַעְתִּי אֶת־יִשְׂרָאֵל וָאֶזְכֹּר אֶת־בְּרִיתִי (Exod. 6.5)

c. שָׁמַע יִשְׂרָאֵל וְאָהַבְתָּ אֵת יהוה (Deut. 6.4-5)

d. תִּשְׁמֹר אֶת־מִצְוֹת יְהוָה וְהָלַכְתָּ בִּדְרָכָיו (Deut. 28.9)

e. לֹא־סָר מֵאַחֲרָיו וַיִּשְׁמֹר מִצְוֹתָיו (2 Kgs 18.6; סָר is Qal perfect 3ms from סוּר)

LESSON 21

Niphal

21.1. *The Nun Prefix*

It will be remembered from as far back as Lesson 14 that the simple verb stem is known as the Qal form. Grammarians refer to the other, that is, nonsimple, stems as *derived* stems. The first of these so-called derived stems to be discussed is the Niphal stem. It is characterized by the feature of a nun (נ) prefixed to a verb's base forms. More on this later.

21.2. *The Function of Niphal*

A fundamental function of the derived stem Niphal is to express a reflexive action—an action that a subject performs upon itself. Examples of strong verbs in Niphal include: נִשְׁמְרוּ 'they guarded themselves'; הִסָּתֵר 'hide yourself'.

The Niphal form can also be used to denote the passive voice of Qal, whose voice is active (recall Lesson 14.2): נִלְכַּדְתְּ 'you were captured'; אֶקָּבֵר 'I will be buried'.

In some verbal roots where no Qal forms exist in the Bible, the Niphal has an active meaning similar to the hypothetical Qal form: נִרְדָּם 'sleeping deeply'.

Note that whether reflexive, passive or neither, Niphal's kind and time of action is comparable in range to that of Qal.

21.3. *Niphal Perfect and Participle*

As hinted above, the Niphal stem attaches a nun to a verb's root letters to make the *perfect* tense, third person, masculine gender, singular number: for example, נ + זהר = נִזְהַר. The šᵉwâ is silent (that is, a syllable divider) so that the syllable starting with nun is closed—here and throughout the perfect paradigm. The inflectional sufformatives for Niphal are identical to those for Qal.

3ms	נִקְטַל	3cp	נִקְטְלוּ
3fs	נִקְטְלָה		
2ms	נִקְטַלְתָּ	2mp	נִקְטַלְתֶּם
2fs	נִקְטַלְתְּ	2fp	נִקְטַלְתֶּן
1cs	נִקְטַלְתִּי	1cp	נִקְטַלְנוּ

Notice that Niphal perfect 3fs is identical in form to Qal cohortative 1cp. Context will help you decide between them.

The Niphal *participle* is based on the Niphal perfect.

ms	*נִקְטָל	mp	נִקְטָלִים
fs	*נִקְטָלָה / נִקְטֶלֶת	fp	נִקְטָלוֹת

[*Distinguish carefully between the perfects נִקְטַל (3ms) and נִקְטְלָה (3fs), on the one hand, and the participles נִקְטָל (ms) and נִקְטָלָה (fs), on the other.]

21.4. Niphal Imperfect and Imperative

In the *imperfect* tense the nun prefix of Niphal assimilates to the following consonant—that is, to the first letter of the root form. Thus, a dagesh forte shows up in every imperfect form: for example, יִלָּחֵם from hypothetical יִנְלָחֵם. Like the perfect, the imperfect employs the same preformatives and sufformatives in Niphal as in Qal.

3ms	יִקָּטֵל	3mp	יִקָּטְלוּ
3fs	תִּקָּטֵל	3fp	תִּקָּטַלְנָה
2ms	תִּקָּטֵל	2mp	תִּקָּטְלוּ
2fs	תִּקָּטְלִי	2fp	תִּקָּטַלְנָה
1cs	*אֶקָּטֵל	1cp	נִקָּטֵל

[*Or אִקָּטֵל with ḥireq—the vowel always found in Niphal cohortative 1cs, אִקָּטְלָה.]

Observe that the vowel before the final syllable (נָה) in the feminine plurals is pataḥ.

The appearance of the Niphal *imperatives* differs from the second-person Niphal imperfects only by substituting he for taw.

ms	הִקָּטֵל	mp	הִקָּטְלוּ
fs	הִקָּטְלִי	fp	הִקָּטַלְנָה

21.5. *Niphal Infinitives*

As in the Qal stem, so in the Niphal stem the *infinitive construct* shares the masculine singular imperative form: that is, הִקָּטֵל. An infinitive construct may assume a pronominal suffix (see Lesson 19.4): for example, הִשָּׁעֶנְךָ 'your relying'.

The *infinitive absolute* splits its occurrences among הִקָּטֵל (the shape of the construct), הִקָּטֹל (with ḥōlem), and נִקְטֹל (similar to the perfect). The forms with He tend to pair off with imperfect finite verbs while the form with nun tends to pair off with perfect finite verbs:

אִם־הִפָּקֵד יִפָּקֵד	'if he is missing' (1 Kgs 20.39)
נִשְׁאֹל נִשְׁאַל	'he earnestly requested for himself' (1 Sam. 20.6)

Vocabulary

אָסַף	'to gather'
אֲרוֹן	'ark'
בֹּקֶר	'morning'
יָשַׁע (הוֹשִׁיעַ Hiphil)	'to save'
כָּלָה	'to be finished'
נָטָה	'to turn aside; extend'
עָזַב	'to leave'
צַדִּיק	'righteous'
שָׁכַב	'to lie down'
שָׁפַט	'to judge'

Exercises

1. Write the complete inflectional pattern for סתר in the Niphal perfect and Niphal imperfect (compare the exercises in Lessons 14 and 15, respectively). Also show the forms for סתר in the Niphal imperative, infinitive construct and absolute and participle.

2. Translate the following five clauses.
    a. נִמְצְאוּ דְבָרֶיךָ (Jer. 15.16)
    b. וּלְהִלָּחֵם מִלְחֲמֹתֵנוּ (2 Chron. 32.8)
    c. זִבְחֵי אֱלֹהִים רוּחַ נִשְׁבָּרָה (Ps. 51.19)
    d. וַיִּקָּבֵר עִם־אֲבֹתָיו (1 Kgs 14.31)
    e. וְלֹא־יִקָּרֵא עוֹד אֶת־שִׁמְךָ אַבְרָם (Gen. 17.5; hint: אֵת can mark the subject of a passive verb)

LESSON 22

Piel, Pual

22.1. *The Functions of Piel and Pual*
The Piel and Pual stems defy easy classification according to function. However, a number of main nuances can be identified:

1. A factitive role can be seen in both Piel and Pual. In the active voice (which Piel represents) factitive more often than not means 'to make to *be* something'. In the passive voice (which Pual represents) factitive more often than not means 'to be made to *be* something'. For example: whereas in Qal גדל translates 'to be great', in Piel גדל translates 'to make to be great, or to exalt'; while in Qal טמא means 'to be unclean', in Piel טמא means 'to make/declare to be unclean, or to pollute'; whereas in Qal קדש reads 'to be holy,' in Pual קדש reads 'to be made to be holy, or to be sanctified'.*

[*'To make to *do* something' or 'to be made to *do* something' we may prefer to designate causative (as opposed to factitive). While the Hiphil and Hophal stems (discussed in the next lesson) generally express causation, Piel and Pual can also carry this nuance: for example, אבד in Qal translates 'to perish' while in Piel means 'to make/cause to perish, or to destroy'; למד in Qal means 'to learn' while in Pual means 'to be made/ caused to learn, or to be taught'.]

2. An intensive action is also to be recognized. The intensive notion has to do with the pluralization or the frequency of an action. For example: whereas in Qal שבר reads 'to break', in Piel שבר reads 'to break into pieces'; while in Qal רנן means 'to shout', in Pual רנן means 'to be shouted repeatedly'.

3. A denominative nuance can also be observed. Denominative Piels and Puals are closer in meaning to some nouns or adjectives than to a Qal verb (which in many cases does not

exist). For example: Piel אלם meaning 'to bind sheaves' is derived from the noun אֲלֻמָּה 'sheaf'; Piel שרש meaning 'to uproot' is derived from the noun שֹׁרֶשׁ 'root'; Pual דבר meaning 'to be spoken' is derived from the noun דָּבָר 'word'.

22.2. *The Form of Piel and Pual*

A doubling of the middle root consonant distinguishes Piel and Pual from Qal: for example, שַׁלַּח (Piel infinitive); מְחַטֵּא (Piel participle); סֻפַּר (Pual perfect). The characteristic dagesh forte sometimes disappears from the second root letter when it carries a vocal šᵉwâ (remember Lesson 4.2): for example, הַלְלוּ (Piel imperative) instead of הַלְּלוּ. Naturally, since every preformative in the Piel and Pual imperfect contains a vocal šᵉwâ, the waw consecutive can lose its dagesh forte when attached to an imperfect from these stems: for example, וַיְזַנֵּב instead of וַיְּזַנֵּב.

The forms of the imperative, infinitives and participle are largely predictable from the imperfect. The perfect is quite different.

22.3. *Piel*

As mentioned above, Piel is active. Its *perfect* conjugation follows:

3ms	קִטֵּל	3cp	קִטְּלוּ
3fs	קִטְּלָה		
2ms	קִטַּלְתָּ	2mp	קִטַּלְתֶּם
2fs	קִטַּלְתְּ	2fp	קִטַּלְתֶּן
1cs	קִטַּלְתִּי	1cp	קִטַּלְנוּ

Notice that ḥireq stands beneath the initial consonant throughout the inflection. You will discover that even the third masculine singular of the perfect in Piel verbs may have a pataḥ instead of ṣērê in the second syllable: for example, גִּדַּל. There are also instances of sᵉgōl ousting ṣērê in 3ms: for example, כִּבֶּס.

Piel *imperfects* appear thus:

3ms	יְקַטֵּל	3mp	יְקַטְּלוּ
3fs	תְּקַטֵּל	3fp	תְּקַטֵּלְנָה
2ms	תְּקַטֵּל	2mp	תְּקַטְּלוּ
2fs	תְּקַטְּלִי	2fp	תְּקַטֵּלְנָה
1cs	אֲקַטֵּל	1cp	נְקַטֵּל

Unlike Niphal, Piel retains a ṣērê in the syllable before נָה (3fp and 2fp).

The *imperative* is basically a shortened form of the imperfect:

ms	קַטֵּל	mp	קַטְּלוּ
fs	קַטְּלִי	fp	קַטֵּלְנָה

A Begadkefat letter at the beginning of an imperative must receive dagesh lene: for example, דַּבֵּר.

The *infinitive construct* assumes the same shape as imperative masculine singular: that is, קַטֵּל. While in the majority of cases the *infinitive absolute* follows this basic pattern, divergence is attested: hence, either קַטֵּל or קַטֹּל.

Participles exhibit a stem prefix of mem.

ms	מְקַטֵּל	mp	מְקַטְּלִים
fs	מְקַטְּלָה / מְקַטֶּלֶת	fp	מְקַטְּלוֹת

22.4. *Piel with Pronominal Suffixes*
Like Qal verbs, Piel verbs can take objective—that is, direct object—pronominal suffixes (see Lesson 19).

אֱלֹהַי פַּלְּטֵנִי מִיַּד רָשָׁע	'O my God, rescue me from the hand of the wicked' (Ps. 71.4)
גַּדֶּלְךָ בְּעֵינֵי כָל־יִשְׂרָאֵל	'to make you great in all Israel's eyes' (Josh. 3.7)
וְחִטְּאוֹ בַּיּוֹם הַשְּׁבִיעִי	'and he will free him from sin on the seventh day' (Num. 19.19)

22.5. *Pual*
Being passive, Pual verbs cannot take suffixed pronouns which indicate direct objects.

The paradigm for the Pual *perfect* is as follows.

3ms	קֻטַּל	3cp	קֻטְּלוּ
3fs	קֻטְּלָה		
2ms	קֻטַּלְתָּ	2mp	קֻטַּלְתֶּם
2fs	קֻטַּלְתְּ	2fp	קֻטַּלְתֶּן
1cs	קֻטַּלְתִּי	1cp	קֻטַּלְנוּ

Observe how qibbûṣ consistently appears in the opening syllable. Apart from this feature, and the fact that 3ms Piel has a ṣērê as the vowel of the second syllable, Pual perfect looks like Piel perfect.

The *imperfect* Pual also shows qibbûṣ under its initial root consonant.

3ms	יְקֻטַּל	3mp	יְקֻטְּלוּ
3fs	תְּקֻטַּל	3fp	תְּקֻטַּלְנָה
2ms	תְּקֻטַּל	2mp	תְּקֻטְּלוּ
2fs	תְּקֻטְּלִי	2fp	תְּקֻטַּלְנָה
1cs	אֲקֻטַּל	1cp	נְקֻטַּל

Pual has no imperative forms. Surprisingly, no infinitive construct is attested. Only a single *infinitive absolute* is extant in the Hebrew Bible: namely גֻּנֹּב.

The *participle* conforms to this model:

ms	מְקֻטָּל	mp	מְקֻטָּלִים
fs	מְקֻטָּלָה / מְקֻטֶּלֶת	fp	מְקֻטָּלוֹת

Vocabulary

בְּהֵמָה	'animal'
גָּלָה	'to uncover, reveal'
חָצֵר	'settlement, court'
יָכֹל	'to be able'
כָּבוֹד	'glory, honor'
כַּף	'palm; sole'
לָכֵן	'therefore'
רֵעַ	'friend'
שֵׁבֶט	'rod; tribe'
שֶׁמֶן	'oil'

Exercises

Translate the clauses and parse the verbs in the following verses. Include any waw consecutives encountered under the heading *other feature* (compare the exercise section of Lesson 19).

a. כִּי עַתָּה שָׁלַחְתִּי אֵלֶיךָ (Dan. 10.11)

b. בְּיַד מְבַקְשֵׁי נַפְשָׁם (Jer. 46.26)

c. לְמַלֵּא אֶת־דְּבַר יְהוָה (1 Kgs 2.27)

d. לַמֶּדְנָה בְנוֹתֵיכֶם נֶהִי (Jer. 9.19; this sentence reveals how masculine pronominal suffixes—either objective or possessive—refer not infrequently to feminine antecedents, particularly in the plural)

e. כְּדַבְּרָהּ אֶל־יוֹסֵף יוֹם יוֹם (Gen. 39.10)

f. יְהַלְלוּ שְׁמוֹ בְמָחוֹל (Ps. 149.3)

g. וַיְשַׁבֵּר אֹתָם (Exod. 32.19)

LESSON 23

Hiphil, Hophal

23.1. *The Functions of Hiphil and Hophal*

Hiphil and Hophal derived stems, like Piel and Pual forms, are used to express a variety of nuances. These senses may be summarized as follows:*

1. Hiphil verbs normally serve as the causative of Qal verbs; Hophal acts as a passive counterpart to Hiphil, which is active. While בָּרַךְ translates 'to kneel' in Qal, בָּרַךְ translates 'to cause to kneel' in Hiphil; whereas שָׁכַב reads 'to lie down' in Qal, שָׁכַב reads 'to cause to lie down' in Hiphil and 'to be caused to lie down' in Hophal.

2. However, Hiphil and Hophal verbs are sometimes used in factitive or declarative senses like Piels and Puals: whereas כָּבֵד means 'to be heavy' in Qal, כָּבֵד means 'to make to be heavy' in Hiphil; while רָשַׁע translates 'to be guilty' in Qal, רָשַׁע translates 'to declare to be guilty' in Hiphil.

3. Some Hiphil and Hophal verbs have meanings along the lines of Qal verbs: that is, simple rather than causative or factitive/declarative. Quite often no Qal forms occur in the Masoretic Text: Qal lacks לבן, which denotes 'to be white' in Hiphil; similarly, there is no Qal form of חבא, which denotes 'to keep hidden' in Hiphil and 'to be kept hidden' in Hophal.

[*These categories, of course, do not exhaust the possibilities for the two stems. Many Hiphil and Hophal verbs must remain unclassified with regard to signification.]

23.2. *The Form of Hiphil and Hophal*

The distinctive mark of the Hiphil and Hophal conjugations is a pre-fixed he—which appears though merely on the perfect, imperative and infinitives: הָחְתֵּל (Hophal infinitive absolute)*; הַשְׁמִיעוּ (Hiphil imperative); הִרְחַקְתָּ (Hiphil perfect).

The forms of Hiphil and Hophal imperfect and participle are to be discerned by means of the respective vowel patterns (see below).

[*Note that throughout Hiphil and Hophal, dagesh lene will be present in a root's middle letter whenever it is a Begadkefat.]

23.3. *Hiphil*

The stem prefix he in Hiphil *perfect* bears the vowel ḥireq. An initial root consonant combines with this הַ to produce a closed syllable.

3ms	הִקְטִיל	3cp	הִקְטִילוּ
3fs	הִקְטִילָה		
2ms	הִקְטַלְתָּ	2mp	הִקְטַלְתֶּם
2fs	הִקְטַלְתְּ	2fp	הִקְטַלְתֶּן
1cs	הִקְטַלְתִּי	1cp	הִקְטַלְנוּ

Just as in Piel the vowel in the second syllable of the Hiphil perfect changes to pataḥ across first and second person forms. Since the addition of vocalic sufformatives to the Hiphil stem does not draw the accent away from the second syllable (contrast Qal, Niphal, Piel, Pual), the ḥireq yōd remains unchanged in 3fs and 3cp, thereby rejecting substitution by vocal šᵉwâ.

In Hiphil the he prefix of the *imperative* is vocalized with pataḥ.

ms	הַקְטֵל	mp	הַקְטִילוּ
fs	הַקְטִילִי	fp	הַקְטֵלְנָה

Before pronominal suffixes the masculine singular Hiphil imperative retains ḥireq yōd: for example, הַזְכִּירֵנִי.

Similarly the *infinitive construct* (הַקְטִיל) and *infinitive absolute* (הַקְטֵל or הַקְטֵיל) have pataḥ under the he.

Pataḥ in the preformative syllable and ḥireq yōd in the second syllable characterize the Hiphil *imperfect*:

3ms	יַקְטִיל	3mp	יַקְטִילוּ
3fs	תַּקְטִיל	3fp	תַּקְטֵלְנָה
2ms	תַּקְטִיל	2mp	תַּקְטִילוּ
2fs	תַּקְטִילִי	2fp	תַּקְטֵלְנָה
1cs	אַקְטִיל	1cp	נַקְטִיל

Ṣērê replaces ḥireq yōd in both feminine plural forms. Instead of becoming šᵉwâ, ḥireq yōd persists in both masculine plurals and in second feminine singular. It does the same thing in cohortatives: that is, אֶקְטִילָה (1cs), נַקְטִילָה (1cp).

Hiphil is the only stem which alters (or 'shortens') its shape for an imperfect consecutive or a jussive (Lessons 16.3 and 20.3) among strong verbs. Thus, for instance, תַּקְטִיל shortens to תַּקְטֵל. Usually, however, there is no reduction for 1cs, which simply keeps its form אַקְטִיל.

The Hiphil *participle* accepts a mem prefix as do Piel and Pual participles. Punctuation will distinguish the latter two from Hiphil, which follows:

ms	מַקְטִיל	mp	מַקְטִילִים
fs	מַקְטִילָה / מַקְטֶלֶת	fp	מַקְטִילוֹת

23.4. *Hiphil with Pronominal Suffixes*
Hiphil verbs share with Qal and Piel verbs the ability to take objective pronominal suffixes:

קָרוֹב מַצְדִּיקִי	'My vindicator is near' (Isa. 50.8)
אַל־תַּשְׁלִיכֵנִי מִלְּפָנֶיךָ	'Do not dismiss me from your presence' (Ps. 51.13)
וְהִשְׁמִידְךָ מֵעַל פְּנֵי הָאֲדָמָה	'and he will destroy you from the face of the earth' (Deut. 6.15)

23.5. *Hophal*
The stem prefix he in Hophal *perfect* carries either the vowel qāmeṣ qāṭān or less frequently qibbûṣ. The syllable including הָ / הֻ + a root's first letter is closed.

3ms	הָקְטַל	3cp	הָקְטְלוּ
3fs	הָקְטְלָה		
2ms	הָקְטַלְתָּ	2mp	הָקְטַלְתֶּם
2fs	הָקְטַלְתְּ	2fp	הָקְטַלְתֶּן
1cs	הָקְטַלְתִּי	1cp	הָקְטַלְנוּ

Pataḥ surfaces in the second syllable of all forms except 3fs and 3cp, where vocal šᵉwâ arises.

Hophal by its passive nature has no imperative. Coincidentally, an infinitive construct is attested for no strong verb. The *infinitive absolute* (הָקְטֵל) imitates the perfect's he prefix with qāmeṣ qāṭān.

Imperfects also exhibit either a qāmeṣ qāṭān or a qibbûṣ in the opening syllable and generally display a pataḥ in the succeeding syllable.

3ms	יִקְטַל	3mp	יִקְטְלוּ
3fs	תָּקְטַל	3fp	תָּקְטַלְנָה
2ms	תָּקְטַל	2mp	תָּקְטְלוּ
2fs	תָּקְטְלִי	2fp	תָּקְטַלְנָה
1cs	אָקְטַל	1cp	נָקְטַל

In Hophal *participles* the stem prefix mem prefers qibbûṣ over qāmeṣ qāṭān. Between the second and third consonants of the verb root will be qāmeṣ gādôl/rāḥāb.

| ms | מָקְטָל | mp | מָקְטָלִים |
| fs | מָקְטָלָה / מָקְטֶלֶת | fp | מָקְטָלוֹת |

Vocabulary

אָבַד	'to perish'
אֹזֶן	'ear'
אֶפְרַיִם	'Ephraim'
בָּקָר	'cattle'
זָקֵן	'old'
יַרְדֵּן	'Jordan'
מוֹאָב	'Moab'
מִצְוָה	'commandment'
סֵפֶר	'book'
שָׁבַע (Niphal נִשְׁבַּע)	'to swear'

Exercises

Find the following sentences in the Hebrew Bible and translate them. I offer words 3 to 5 of Isa. 9.2 as an example.

לֹא הִגְדַּלְתָּ הַשִּׂמְחָה   'You have made joy for it great'*

[*This illustration affords me the chance to introduce a phenomenon called *kethib-qere* (or *qere-kethib*). On checking the text printed in the Hebrew Bible, it will be seen that לֹא has a small circle resting over it. The circle directs your attention to the margin of the page where the letters לו are printed with qoph either beneath or behind those letters. The Masoretes (remember Lesson 3.1) are thereby indicating that, in their opinion, the consonants לא were written (*kethib*) erroneously and the consonants לו + the vowel ḥōlem should be read (*qere*). Reverence for the text prevented scribes from changing it other than in their marginal notes. You will meet the *kethib-qere* feature throughout the Hebrew Bible.]

    a. Jer. 39.2: final pair of words

    b. Ps. 22.16: word with 'atnāḥ and the two words preceding it
        (three terms in total)

c. Isa. 63.7: first three terms
d. Ezek. 14.19: last eight words
e. Deut. 31.17: seventh to ninth terms (in other words, skip the first six and work on the next three)
f. Lev. 21.8: term with 'atnāḥ and the three before it (four words in total)
g. Jer. 5.20: skip over the last word and translate the two ahead of it

LESSON 24

Hithpael

24.1. *The Function of Hithpael*

Hithpael verbs, which appear with relative infrequency in the Hebrew Bible, are intransitive—that is, they do not take direct objects (including objective pronominal suffixes).

Generally speaking, Hithpael verbs carry a basic reflexive meaning (compare Niphal). This nuance is often attested with root forms that are found elsewhere in the active (that is, verbs in Qal, Piel or Hiphil). The basic reflexive becomes reciprocal when each member of a group does something concerning the rest of the group. Indirect reflexive—that is, doing something to one's own advantage or disadvantage—belongs here too. Biblical examples include:

וְיִתְגַּדֵּל עַל־כָּל־אֵל	'And he will exalt himself above every god' (simple reflexive) (Dan. 11.36)
לָמָּה תִּתְרָאוּ	'Why do you look at each other?' (reciprocal) (Gen. 42.1)*
אֶל־הַמֶּלֶךְ לְהִתְחַנֶּן־לוֹ	'to the king to implore favor from him' (indirect reflexive) (Est. 4.8)

[*תִּתְרָאוּ derives from רָאָה, a verb attesting features of both ayin–guttural (Lesson 29) and lamedh–he (Lesson 33).]

Additionally Hithpael verbs can (1) have the sense of an intensive; (2) develop into a pure passive; (3) have the nuance of a pretensive (that is, disguising oneself as such and such); or (4) arise as a denominative. Examples from the Hebrew Bible help to illustrate:

אֶתְהַלֵּךְ לִפְנֵי יְהוָה	'I walk constantly before Yahweh' (intensive) (Ps. 116.9)
וְיִשְׁתַּכְּחוּ בָעִיר	'And they are forgotten in the city' (passive) (Eccl. 8.10)

הִתְאַבְּלִי־נָא   'Please feign to be a mourner!' (pretensive) (2 Sam. 14.2)
בְּנוֹת עַמְּךָ הַמִּתְנַבְּאוֹת מִלִּבְּהֶן   'your people's daughters who prophesy
out of their imagination' (denominative)
(Ezek. 13.17)

24.2. *The Form of Hithpael*
Perfects, imperatives, and infinitives in Hithpael prefix the closed
syllable הִת to the verbal root. The stem prefix for participles is the
closed syllable מִת. We might say that imperfects *infix* a taw after the
preformatives (more will be said about this later).

A doubled second root consonant characterizes Hithpael; regularly a
ṣērê is found under that letter. Occasionally the ṣērê fails to surface in
any Hithpael form of a particular verb. In such cases a pataḥ occurs in
place of ṣērê: for example, יִתְאַנַּף rather than יִתְאַנֵּף.

24.3. *Metathesis and Assimilation*
When the taw of the Hithpael's stem prefix/infix precedes any of the
sibilants (*s* sounds) samekh or sin or shin, the sibilant and the taw regularly exchange positions or metathesize: מִתְסַתֵּר becoming מִסְתַּתֵּר;
הִתְשָׂרֵעַ becoming הִשְׂתָּרֵעַ.*

[*שָׂרַע is a doubly weak verb, being ayin–guttural (Lesson 29) along with lamedh–
guttural (Lesson 31).]

The process is carried still further if the initial root letter is ṣade. Not
only does transposition happen, but also the taw turns into teth: for
example; נִתְצַדָּק becoming נִצְטַדָּק (pausal forms in this instance)
   The taw normally assimilates to the first consonant of a verb whenever that consonant is daleth, teth or another taw: for example, יִתְדַּכָּא
becoming יִדַּכָּא. Assimilation sporadically takes place even with other
letters: for example, הִתְנַבָּאוּ becoming הִנַּבָּאוּ.

24.4. *Inflections of Hithpael*
In the inflection of the *perfect* we usually encounter pataḥ in the third
syllable. (Sufformatives and stress parallel Qal.)

3ms	הִתְקַטֵּל	3cp	הִתְקַטְּלוּ
3fs	הִתְקַטְּלָה		
2ms	הִתְקַטַּלְתָּ	2mp	הִתְקַטַּלְתֶּם
2fs	הִתְקַטַּלְתְּ	2fp	הִתְקַטַּלְתֶּן
1cs	הִתְקַטַּלְתִּי	1cp	הִתְקַטַּלְנוּ

The *imperfect* is characterized by an infixed taw which closes each syllable opened by a preformative.

3ms	יִתְקַטֵּל	3mp	יִתְקַטְּלוּ
3fs	תִּתְקַטֵּל	3fp	תִּתְקַטֵּלְנָה
2ms	תִּתְקַטֵּל	2mp	תִּתְקַטְּלוּ
2fs	תִּתְקַטְּלִי	2fp	תִּתְקַטֵּלְנָה
1cs	אֶתְקַטֵּל	1cp	נִתְקַטֵּל

Note that only 1cs alters its preformative vowel from ḥireq.

Like Niphal, Hithpael *imperative* simply changes the taw of the imperfect second person forms to a he.

ms	הִתְקַטֵּל	mp	הִתְקַטְּלוּ
fs	הִתְקַטְּלִי	fp	הִתְקַטֵּלְנָה

The *infinitive construct* (הִתְקַטֵּל) is identical with the masculine singular imperative. Hithpael lacks an infinitive absolute so that the infinitive construct substitutes for it.

Hithpael offers alternate *participial* forms for feminine singular just like the other stems.

ms	מִתְקַטֵּל	mp	מִתְקַטְּלִים
fs	מִתְקַטְּלָה / מִתְקַטֶּלֶת	fp	מִתְקַטְּלוֹת

Vocabulary

בָּחַר	'to choose'
בִּנְיָמִן	'Benjamin'
בַּעַל	'lord, husband'
חָוָה (Hishtafel הִשְׁתַּחֲוָה)	'to bow down' (this stem is so rare in Hebrew that חוה is the sole root found in Hishtafel)
לָחַם	'to fight'
קָדַשׁ	'to be holy'
רוּם	'to be high'
רָעָה	'to tend (flocks)'
שָׂפָה	'lip'
שָׁאַל	'to ask'

Exercises

1. Draw a line from every word on the left to its synonym on the right.

אֵל	אָדוֹן
בַּעַל	כֹּה
כֵּן	לֹא
נָטָה	סוּר
קָרֵב	תָּוֶךְ

2. Draw a line from every term on the left to its antonym on the right.

חָיָה	אֹיֵב
לַיְלָה	טוֹב
לָקַח	יוֹם
רַע	מוּת
רֵעַ	נָתַן

3. Parse completely the following verbs (remembering to note any special/other features, as instructed back in Lessons 19 and 22).

יְלַמֵּדוּן (in pause)	לְהִלָּחֵם
כָּתוּב	הֻשְׁבַּרְתִּי (in pause)
מְדֻבָּר	הִתְיַצְּבָה (in pause)*

[*This form could represent either of two inflections. You need identify only one of them.]

LESSON 25

Weak Verbs, Pe–Guttural

25.1. *Weak Verbs*

Weak verbs deviate from strong verbs due to there being among the root consonants a guttural letter or resh (for example, מָאֵן instead of מַאֵן, from מאן), or else a letter which may quiesce (for example, תִּבְנֶינָה instead of תִּבָּנֶהְנָה, from בנה) or assimilate (for example, מִגַּשׁ instead of מִנְגַּשׁ, from נגשׁ). In each case adjustments must be made to accommodate the changes arising due to the presence of these letters.

Weak verbs fall into ten separate classes. Traditionally they have been described on the basis of a model root פעל, whereby a verb's first letter was considered its pe (פ) consonant, a verb's second letter was considered its ayin (ע) consonant, and a verb's third letter was considered its lamedh (ל) consonant. Many modern grammarians favour designating a first root letter as I, a second as II, and a third as III.

Sample weak verb	Traditional name	Modern name
עמד	pe–guttural*	I–guttural*
אכל	pe–aleph	I–aleph
ברך	ayin–guttural*	II–guttural*
שלח	lamedh–guttural	III–guttural
מצא	lamedh–aleph	III–aleph
נגש	pe–nun	I–nun
ישב	pe–yōd/waw	I–yōd/waw
קום	ayin–yōd/waw	hollow
גלה	lamedh–he	III–He
סבב	double ayin	geminate

[*The label 'guttural' here is utilized expansively to include resh.]

The first five classes or categories above do not under normal circumstances lose consonants; instead vowel changes are attested (thus they are divergent from strong verbs). The last five classes often attest the loss of consonants as well as exhibiting vowel change.

25.2. *Qal Pe–Gutturals*

A pe–guttural verb possesses he, heth, ayin or resh as initial consonant. (Lesson 26 will treat verbs that start with aleph.) It will be remembered that these letters cannot double and generally take compound šᵉwâs.

1. In Qal perfect, only the second person plural forms vary from the standard paradigm by replacing the vocal šᵉwâ with a ḥāṭēp pataḥ: עֲמַדְתֶּם, עֲמַדְתֶּן.
2. Likewise Qal imperatives possess a composite šᵉwâ in masculine singulars and feminine plurals: עֲמֹד, עֲמֹדְנָה.
3. The infinitive construct looks like the masculine singular imperative; when added an inseparable preposition bears a pataḥ: for example, לַעֲמֹד.
4. Qal passive participles, other than masculine singular, show ḥāṭēp pataḥ too: עֲמוּדָה, עֲמוּדִים, עֲמוּדוֹת.
5. The Qal infinitive absolute and active participle adhere to the pattern of the strong verb.

Qal imperfects assume pataḥ as a preformative vowel for action verbs—except in 1cs where the vowel is sᵉgōl. The corresponding compound šᵉwâ, either ḥāṭēp pataḥ or ḥāṭēp sᵉgōl, goes under the guttural—aside from 2fs, 3mp and 2mp, where the guttural takes a full vowel pataḥ. Additionally cohortative 1cp takes pataḥ under the guttural while with 1cs cohortative the full vowel is sᵉgōl: for example, אֶעְמְדָה.

3ms	יַעֲמֹד	3mp	יַעַמְדוּ
3fs	תַּעֲמֹד	3fp	תַּעֲמֹדְנָה
2ms	תַּעֲמֹד	2mp	תַּעַמְדוּ
2fs	תַּעַמְדִי	2fp	תַּעֲמֹדְנָה
1cs	אֶעֱמֹד	1cp	נַעֲמֹד

For stative verbs the preformative is sᵉgōl throughout; the guttural's vowel is ḥāṭēp sᵉgōl apart from 2fs, 3mp and 2mp, where it is sᵉgōl: for example, יֶחֱזַק, תֶּחֶזְקוּ.

There are also several terms that do not cause substitution of a ḥāṭēp vowel for silent šᵉwâ: for example, יֶחְשֹׁב, תֶּהְדַּר.

25.3. *Niphal Pe–Gutturals*

The nun prefix in Niphal perfect uniformly carries sᵉgōl; after the guttural ḥāṭēp sᵉgōl surfaces—except for another sᵉgōl in 3fs and 3cp.

3ms	נֶעֱמַד	3cp	נֶעֶמְדוּ
3fs	נֶעֶמְדָה		
2ms	נֶעֱמַ֫דְתָּ	2mp	נֶעֱמַדְתֶּם
2fs	נֶעֱמַדְתְּ	2fp	נֶעֱמַדְתֶּן
1cs	נֶעֱמַ֫דְתִּי	1cp	נֶעֱמַ֫דְנוּ

The same vowel sequence (sᵉgōl succeeded by ḥāṭēp sᵉgōl) is present in the participle: for example, נֶעֱמָד.

The nun prefix of the Niphal infinitive absolute is pointed with a pataḥ followd by ḥāṭēp pataḥ: for example, נַעֲמוֹד.

Again, certain words abhor a compound šᵉwâ: for example, נֶחְשַׁ֫בְתִּי.

Since the guttural cannot receive the dagesh forte present in the strong verb, the preformative vowel of the Niphal imperfect changes ('lengthens') from ḥireq to ṣērê across the board: for example, תֵּעָמְדוּ. This is also the case for the imperative, infinitive construct and infinitive absolute, which exhibit a ṣērê beneath the he prefix: for example, הֵעָמְדִי, הֵעָמֵד, הֵעָמוֹד.

25.4. *Hiphil Pe–Gutturals*

Consistently the Hiphil perfect prefix vowel is sᵉgōl and guttural vowel is ḥāṭēp sᵉgōl: for example, הֶעֱמִיד. However the order regularly becomes pataḥ + ḥāṭēp pataḥ in the first and second persons following waw consecutive: for example, הֶעֱבַדְתִּיךָ becomes וְהַעֲבַדְתִּיךָ (coincidentally including a suffixed 2ms pronoun here). This latter sequence of vowels is exactly that which occurs in Hiphil imperfects (including cohortatives and jussives), imperatives, infinitives, and participles: אַעֲמִיד (1cs imperfect); יַעֲמֵד (3ms jussive); הַעֲמִ֫ידוּ (mp imperative); הַעֲמִיד (construct infinitive); מַעֲמֶ֫דֶת (fs participle).

A reduced vowel may be rejected here as well: for example, מַחְשִׁיךְ.

25.5. *Hophal Pe–Gutturals*

In Hophal perfect, šᵉwâ beneath the guttural becomes ḥāṭēp qāmeṣ—with the exception of 3fs and 3cp, in which that ḥāṭēp qāmeṣ switches to qāmeṣ qāṭān.

3ms	הָעֳמַד	3cp	הָעֳמְדוּ
3fs	הָעֳמְדָה		
2ms	הָעֳמַ֫דְתָּ	2mp	הָעֳמַדְתֶּם
2fs	הָעֳמַדְתְּ	2fp	הָעֳמַדְתֶּן
1cs	הָעֳמַ֫דְתִּי	1cp	הָעֳמַ֫דְנוּ

Hophal imperfects similarly replace simple šᵉwâ with ḥāṭēp qāmeṣ, other than where that composite šᵉwâ switches to qāmeṣ Qāṭān in 2fs, 3mp, 2mp.

3ms	יָעֳמַד	3mp	יָעֳמְדוּ
3fs	תָּעֳמַד	3fp	תָּעֳמַ֫דְנָה
2ms	תָּעֳמַד	2mp	תָּעֳמְדוּ
2fs	תָּעֳמְדִי	2fp	תָּעֳמַ֫דְנָה
1cs	אָעֳמַד	1cp	נָעֳמַד

Both infinitive absolute and participle manifest ḥāṭēp qāmeṣ in place of šᵉwâ; the participial mem prefix always holds qāmeṣ qāṭān (not qibbûṣ): for example, מָעֳמָדוֹת, הָעֳמֵד.* (The infinitive construct is absent from the Masoretic Text.)

[*The sound at the beginning of these two illustrations and of all forms in this section is qāmeṣ qāṭān rather than qāmeṣ gādôl.]

Note that pe–guttural verbs in Piel, Pual and Hithpael are written identically to strong verbs of those stems.

Exercises

(From this point onwards, exercises will require the translation of extended passages from Scripture rather than isolated phrases or clauses as up until now. In addition you must analyze/parse one verb from each verse. If a verse lacks a verbal form, this is obviously not possible. Conversely, where two or more verbs are present you should parse only the one of your choice.)

Render Gen. 12.4-9 into English and perform verbal analysis. For example:

וְאֶעֶשְׂךָ לְגוֹי גָּדוֹל וַאֲבָרֶכְךָ וַאֲגַדְּלָה שְׁמֶךָ וֶהְיֵה בְּרָכָה	'Then I will make you into a great nation and bless you and magnify your name; as for you, be a blessing!' (Gen. 12.2).

וְהְיֵה = Qal imperative masculine singular from היה, with a waw con-junction. (If this verse had been assigned to you, I would have penned a reading note telling you to interpret וְהְיֵה as if spelled וִהְיֵה, which is the shape strong verbs take. I would also have supplied reading notes for the first and fourth words—both weak verbs of a class not yet studied.)

Reading Notes on Genesis 12.4-9

Verse 4:

וַיֵּלֶךְ	Interpret as if spelled וַיִּהְלֹךְ (הלך behaves like pe–yōd/waw verbs [Lesson 28])
בְּצֵאתוֹ	Interpret as if spelled בְּיְצָאוֹ (יצא is both pe–yōd/waw and lamedh–aleph [Lesson 32])

Verse 5:

וַיִּקַּח	Interpret as if spelled וַיִּלְקַח (לקח acts similarly to pe–nun verbs [Lesson 27] along with being lamedh–gut-tural [Lesson 31])
רָכָשׁוּ	In pause, so that the second qāmeṣ is ousting a šᵉwâ
עָשׂוּ	Interpret as if spelled עָשְׂהוּ (עשה is lamedh–he [Lesson 33] besides pe–guttural)
וַיֵּצְאוּ	Interpret as if spelled וַיְיְצָאוּ
לָלֶכֶת	Interpret as if spelled לִהְלֶךְ
וַיָּבֹאוּ	Interpret as if spelled וַיִּבְוֹאוּ (בוא is hollow [Lesson 30] along with lamedh–aleph)

Verse 7:

וַיֵּרָא	Interpret as if spelled וַיִּרְאֶה (ראה is ayin–guttural [Lesson 29] and lamedh–he besides pe–guttural)
וַיֹּאמֶר	Interpret as if spelled וַיְּאֹמֶר (אמר is pe–aleph [Lesson 26])
אֶתֵּן	Interpret as if spelled אֶנְתֵּן (נתן is pe–nun but also acts like pe–yōd/waw verbs)
וַיִּבֶן	Interpret as if spelled וַיִּבְנֹה (בנה is lamedh–he)
הַנִּרְאֶה	Interpret as if spelled הַנִּרְאֶה

Verse 8:

וַיֵּט   Interpret as if spelled וַיִּנְטֹה (נטה is both pe–nun and
lamedh–he)

וַיִּקְרָא   Interpret as if spelled וַיִּקְרֹא (קרא is ayin–guttural as
well as lamedh–aleph)

Verse 9:

וַיִּסַּע   Interpret as if spelled וַיִּנְסֹע (נסע is both pe–nun and
lamedh–guttural)

LESSON 26

Pe–Aleph

26.1. Likeness to Pe–Guttural

A verbal root beginning with an aleph consonant is a pe–aleph verb. Most of the verbs within this category are conjugated quite similarly to other pe–guttural verbs. (After all an aleph is a guttural letter.) pe–alephs and pe–gutturals are exactly alike in Niphal, Hiphil, and Hophal.* This similarity is found also in the Qal perfect and passive participle: that is, a ḥāṭēp pataḥ under the initial aleph/guttural of both 2mp and 2fp in Qal perfect and of fs, mp and fp in Qal passive participle.

[*Keep in mind that pe–aleph and pe–guttural words in Piel, Pual, and Hithpael completely mimic the strong verb. This is true also in Qal active participle and infinitive absolute. (Consult Lesson 25.)]

26.2. Imperative and Infinitive

Qal imperative forms of pe–aleph roots differ from pe–gutturals by placing a ḥāṭēp seġōl—rather than ḥāṭēp pataḥ—in the first syllable of ms and fp: אֱכֹל, אֱכֹלְנָה.

A pe–aleph infinitive construct assumes the same form as imperative masculine singular; when joined by an inseparable preposition, that preposition has the vowel seġōl (not pataḥ as with pe–guttural): for example, בֶּאֱכֹל.* With pronominal suffixes appended to an infinitive, however, those forms bearing a compound šewâ will usually prefer ḥāṭēp pataḥ over ḥāṭēp seġōl: for example, אָכְלְךָ.

[*Lesson 8.1 introduced how ל + אָמֹר yields לֵאמֹר instead of לֶאֱמֹר with a silent aleph.]

26.3. Imperfect

One group of pe–aleph verbs also shows seġōl instead of pataḥ after the Qal imperfect preformative as well as ḥāṭēp seġōl instead of ḥāṭēp pataḥ after the root aleph. (Only stative pe–guttural roots otherwise possess this s^{e}gōl + ḥāṭēp s^{e}gōl sequence in Qal imperfect.) Surprisingly in 2fs, 3mp and 2mp of Qal imperfect, two paṭaḥs emerge beneath the preformative and aleph in pe–alephs—just as in pe–guttural action verbs.

3ms	יֶאֱזֹר	3mp	יַאַזְרוּ
3fs	תֶּאֱזֹר	3fp	תֶּאֱזֹרְנָה
2ms	תֶּאֱזֹר	2mp	תַּאַזְרוּ
2fs	תַּאַזְרִי	2fp	תֶּאֱזֹרְנָה
1cs	אֶאֱזֹר	1cp	נֶאֱזֹר

In a second set of pe–aleph verbs, the aleph loses its consonantal value in Qal imperfect. This quiescence causes the preformative vowel to become ḥōlem throughout. The sound of the second syllable is generally paṭaḥ.

3ms	יֹאכַל	3mp	יֹאכְלוּ
3fs	תֹּאכַל	3fp	תֹּאכַלְנָה
2ms	תֹּאכַל	2mp	תֹּאכְלוּ
2fs	תֹּאכְלִי	2fp	תֹּאכַלְנָה
1cs	אֹכַל*	1cp	נֹאכַל

[*Here the aleph from the root entirely disappears.]

Observe that Begadkefat letters in the middle of these paradigmatic words contain no dagesh lene since, aleph being silent, a vowel precedes a Begadkefat.

26.4. *Specific Pe–Alephs*

A handful of terms—אָבַד, אָבָה, אָכַל, אָמַר and אָפָה—consistently adhere to the pattern outlined above. However, altered sufformatives attach themselves to the Qal imperfect 2fs, 3mp and 2mp of אבה and אפה, which are lamedh-he verbs (See Lesson 33). In addition, two roots—אָהֵב and אָחֵז—inconsistently present forms with quiescent aleph. Thus it is possible to encounter אֹהַב or תֶּאֱהַב; תֶּאֱחֹז; תֹּאחֵז or יֶאֱהֹז.

When combined with waw consecutive, יֹאמַר, נֹאמַר and תֹּאמַר are replaced by יֹּאמֶר, נֹּאמֶר and תֹּאמֶר respectively. However, when coming immediately before quoted speech (אָמַר means 'to say'), the customary form with paṭaḥ may be used:

וַיֹּאמֶר בָּלָק אֶל־בִּלְעָם מֶה   'Then Balak said to Balaam,
"What…?" ' (Num. 23.11)

וַיֹּאמֶר חֲלֹא אֵת אֲשֶׁר   'And he said, "Is it not that
which…?" ' (Num. 23.12)

אכל is one of just a few Biblical Hebrew verbs that display contours—particularly in the perfect and imperfect tenses—from an obsolete Qal passive stem (compare sections 4 and 5 of Lesson 27). For אכל there is also a participle: namely, אָכֻל, 'eaten, consumed'. The passive Qal stem eventually fell into disuse, perhaps because it was similar in form to Pual perfect and Hophal imperfect.

Exercises
Translate Exod. 3.1-6 and parse one verb from each verse.

Reading Notes on Exodus 3.1-6

Verse 1:

הָיָה   Interpret as if spelled הָיָה (היה is both pe–guttural and lamedh–he)

רֹעֶה   Interpret as if spelled רֹעֶה (רעה is pe–guttural as well as ayin–guttural as well as lamedh–he)

וַיִּנְהַג   Interpret as if spelled וַיִּנְהֹג (נהג is ayin–guttural)

וַיָּבֹא   Interpret as if spelled וַיִּבֹא

Verse 2:

וַיֵּרְא   Interpret as if spelled וַיִּרְאֶה

Verse 3:

אָסֻרָה   Interpret as if spelled אֶסוּרָה (סור is hollow)

וְאֶרְאֶה   Interpret as if spelled וְאֶרְאֶה

יִבְעַר   Interpret as if spelled יִבְעַר (בער is ayin–guttural)

Verse 4:

סָר   Interpret as if spelled סַוָר

לִרְאוֹת   Interpret as if spelled לִרְאוֹה

Verse 5:

שַׁל   Interpret as if spelled נְשַׁל (נשל is pe–nun)

Verse 6:

מֵהַבִּיט   Interpret as if spelled מֵהַנְבִּיט (נבט is pe–nun)

Lesson 27

Pe–Nun

27.1. *Qal*

In the Piel, Pual, and Hithpael stems pe–nun verbs imitate the same pattern as strong verbs. The same is true also in the perfect, infinitive absolute, and participle 'tenses' of the Qal stem. However, in Qal imperfects the nun of the root assimilates to its middle consonant by means of a dagesh forte: for example, the conjugation of נָפַל is:

3ms	יִפֹּל	3mp	יִפְּלוּ
3fs	תִּפֹּל	3fp	תִּפֹּלְנָה
2ms	תִּפֹּל	2mp	תִּפְּלוּ
2fs	תִּפְּלִי	2fp	תִּפֹּלְנָה
1cs	אֶפֹּל	1cp	נִפֹּל

Assimilation is ordinarily avoided when the middle root letter is a guttural, which cannot be double: for example, יִנְהַג (note Lesson 29.2 regarding the pataḥ punctuation).

Stative verbs retaining an *a* vowel in the imperfect forms (Lesson 15.2) show further peculiarities (such as יִגַּשׁ from a hypothetical יִנְגַּשׁ). For one thing, the initial syllable containing nun disappears entirely from the Qal imperative.*

ms	גַּשׁ	mp	גְּשׁוּ
fs	גְּשִׁי	fp	גַּשְׁנָה

In addition, the Qal infinitive construct likewise drops the initial nun but then, as if compensating, tacks a taw on at the close—producing a segolate word: for example, גֶּשֶׁת* rather than נְגֶשׁ. When the preposition לְ is attached to one of the segolate infinitives, the preposition is normally pointed with a qāmeṣ: hence, לָגֶשֶׁת. These construct infinitives with suffixed pronouns prefer ḥireq in the first syllable (see Lesson 19.4): for example, גְּשְׁתוֹ.*

[*A Begadkefat letter at the beginning of an abbreviated imperative or infinitive form of a stative pe–nun verb must bear a dagesh lene.]

27.2. *Niphal*

In some respects Niphal forms reverse the rules governing Qal pe–nun verbs. The imperfect, imperative and infinitive construct of pe–nun terms in Niphal behave according to the strong paradigm. By contrast, the perfect, participle and infinitive absolute deviate; in each case the nun of the root becomes absorbed into the following consonant: נִגַּשְׁנוּ for נִנְגַּשְׁנוּ (perfect); נִגָּשֵׁת for נִנְגָּשֵׁת (participle); נִגּוֹשׁ for נִנְגּוֹשׁ (infinitive absolute).

27.3. *Hiphil and Hophal*

In every part of the pe–nun Hiphil and Hophal, the nun assimilates. So, for instance, הַפֵּלְנָה (Hiphil imperative), הַפֵּל (Hiphil infinitive absolute), אַפִּילָה (Hiphil cohortative), יַפֵּל (Hiphil jussive). And thus, illustratively, הֻפְּלוּ (Hophal perfect), תֻּפְּלִי (Hophal imperfect), הֻפַּל (Hophal infinitive construct), מֻפָּל (Hophal participle). You will observe that Hophals favor qibbûṣ over qāmeṣ qāṭān throughout their inflection whenever they derive from pe–nun roots.

27.4. *Pe–Nun Mimic*

The term לְקַח acts as though pe–nun and stative among Qal forms. This means that in the imperfect the lamedh is incorporated into the qoph: for example, יִקְחוּ.* In the imperative the lamedh falls away: for example, קַח. The infinitive construct loses the lamedh and at the same time gains a taw: that is, קַחַת. (The pataḥs replace sᵉgōls because of the heth [consult Lesson 31 about lamedh–guttural weak verbs].)

[*Here, incidentally, we see how in some imperfect pe–nun verbs, doubling of the second root consonant is abandoned wherever the letter carries šᵉwâ (compare Lesson 4.2): consequently we find יִקְחוּ instead of יִקְּחוּ. This phenomenon can arise in the Qal, Niphal and Hophal forms of the pe–nun verb.]

It is worth commenting in passing that forms like לֻקַּחְתָּ, תֻּקַּח and לֻקַּח are passive Qals (see Lesson 26), being perfect, imperfect and participle respectively.

27.5. Peculiar Pe–Nun

The verb נתן is particularly remarkable for several reasons. In the Qal
and Niphal perfect the final nun of the root always assimilates to the
initial consonant of a sufformative: for example, נָתַתְּ from a theoretical
נָתַנְתְּ; נִתַּנּוּ in place of נִתְנְנוּ. (This latter instance does not actually differ
from what you would have expected in light of what was said in 14.2.)

The Qal imperfect forms of נתן have neither ḥōlem nor pataḥ in their
second syllable; instead we find ṣērê: for example, יִתֵּן, אֶתֵּן. The same
vowel surfaces in the Qal imperative: תֵּן. (Of course the ṣērê can reduce
to a simple šᵉwâ: for example, תְּנִי, יִתְּנוּ.) Rather than תֶּנֶת, which we
might have expected, the Qal infinitive construct becomes תֵּת. Only
twice do we encounter the form נְתֹן, which apparently follows the rules
governing the strong verbal pattern.

A Qal passive appears (as with לקח above) in the imperfect יֻתַּן.

Exercises
For Deut. 6.4-9 continue the translation and analysis routine established
in Lesson 25.

Reading Notes on Deuteronomy 6.4-9

Verse 6:

וְהָיוּ   Interpret as if spelled וְהָיְיהוּ

מְצַוְּךָ   Interpret as if spelled מְצַוְּהֶךָ (צוה is lamedh–he)

Verse 7:

בְּשִׁבְתְּךָ   Interpret as if spelled בְּיִשְׁבְךָ (ישב is pe–yōd/waw)

וּבְלֶכְתְּךָ   Interpret as if spelled וּבְהָלְכְךָ

וּבְקוּמֶךָ   Interpret as if spelled וּבְקָוֺמֶךָ (קום is hollow)

LESSON 28

Pe–Yōd/Waw

28.1. Yōd Versus Waw

There are two distinct types of weak verbs which attest yōd as the first root letter. The first type, represented by such words as יָשַׁר, is to be considered as a true pe–yōd. The other type, represented by such words as יָלַד, comes from an original וְלַד and is therefore to be understood as a pe–waw. To repeat, pe–yōd/waw verbs include all verbs whose lexical forms as they now stand have an initial consonant of yōd—regardless of their historical shape.

28.2. Pe–Waw Qal

We will start by looking at terms originally pe–waw. They follow the established patterns of the strong roots in Qal perfect, infinitive absolute and participle.

Pe–waw action verbs, however, discard the derivative yōd from the Qal imperfect, imperative, and infinitive construct. For example: יֵשֵׁב rather than a hypothetical יִישֵׁב; שֵׁב not שְׁבִי; יִשְׁבִי; לָשֶׁבֶת for לִישֵׁב (listed here with לְ preposition).

Notice how an infinitive construct from a pe–waw action verb parallels an infinitive construct from a pe–nun stative verb. So too imperatives of these forms resemble each other—albeit with action pe–waws having ṣērê wherever stative pe–nuns have pataḥ. (This phenomenon was discussed in Lesson 27.)

ms	שֵׁב	mp	שְׁבוּ
fs	שְׁבִי	fp	שֵׁבְנָה

The imperfect preformative vowel is ṣērê. The second syllable also contains a ṣērê unless it becomes volatilized to šᵉwâ before a vocalic sufformative or becomes altered to pataḥ before the נָה ending.

3ms	יֵשֵׁב	3mp	יֵשְׁבוּ
3fs	תֵּשֵׁב	3fp	תֵּשַׁבְנָה
2ms	תֵּשֵׁב	2mp	תֵּשְׁבוּ
2fs	תֵּשְׁבִי	2fp	תֵּשַׁבְנָה
1cs	אֵשֵׁב	1cp	נֵשֵׁב

A waw consecutive will cause the accent to retract in an imperfect of 3ms, 3fs, 2ms and 1cp (compare Lesson 20.3)—but not 1cs. The ṣērê of the final syllable 'shortens' to a sᵉgōl: for example, וַיֵּשֶׁב .

In pe–waw stative verbs, the root letter yōd quiesces in the Qal imperfect tense without completely dropping out. In other words, the preformative vowel ḥireq captures the yōd to produce a ḥireq yōd: thus, אִירַשׁ instead of אִירַשׁ or instead even of אֵירַשׁ. Like strong stative verbs, pataḥ appears in the second syllable. The stress does not recede after a consecutive waw: for example, וַיִּירַשׁ but not something on the order of וַיִּירֶשׁ.

Imperatives—רְשָׁנָה for instance—and infinitive constructs—רֶשֶׁת— assume contours comparable to pe–waw action verbs (and pe–nun stative verbs). Pe–waw statives mirror strong verbs in perfect and infinitive absolute. (Remember that statives do not have true participles; Lesson 18.2.)

The verb יכל, which belongs to this grouping, has variant forms with šūreq in the Qal imperfect preformative: for example, תּוּכְלוּ. (Perhaps these forms should really be considered Hophals.?) However that might be, the infinitive construct of יכל takes the highly unexpected appearance of יְכֹלֶת.

28.3. *Pe–Waw Niphal*
The derived stems do not distinguish between action verb forms and stative verb forms. In Niphal perfects a ḥōlem waw surfaces in those places where a strong verb would manifest a ḥireq + initial root consonant (in this case yōd) + šᵉwâ.

3ms	נוֹשַׁב	3cp	נוֹשְׁבוּ
3fs	נוֹשְׁבָה		
2ms	נוֹשַׁבְתָּ	2mp	נוֹשַׁבְתֶּם
2fs	נוֹשַׁבְתְּ	2fp	נוֹשַׁבְתֶּן
1cs	נוֹשַׁבְתִּי	1cp	נוֹשַׁבְנוּ

The same phenomenon is also attested with Niphal participles: for example, נוֹשָׁבֹת for feminine plural נִישָׁבוֹת.

In the imperfect, imperative and infinitive forms of the pe–waw verbs the initial yōd reverts to being a waw consonant. In addition, the nun of the Niphal prefix coalesces with that waw to yield a doubled waw, marked by dagesh forte: for example, אִוָּשֵׁב (1cs imperfect); הִוָּשְׁבוּ (mp imperative); הִוָּשֵׁב (construct infinitive); הִוָּשֵׁב (absolute infinitive).

Throughout the inflection of Piel and Pual, pe–waw roots normally retain the contemporary initial yōd as found in dictionary entries. However, the original waw is sometimes preserved in the conjugation of Hithpael: thus, we observe forms with waw, for example יִתְוַכָּח (coincidentally pausal) from יכח or with yōd יִתְיַלְדוּ (notice that the lamedh appears without dagesh; see Lesson 4.2) from ילד.

28.4. *Pe–Waw Hiphil and Hophal*
Pe–nun verbs in the Hiphil inflection regularly substitute הוֹ for הִ as the stem prefix in the perfect tense and הוֹ for הַ in the imperative as well as infinitive absolute and construct: הוֹשַׁבְתְּ (perfect 2fs); הוֹשִׁיבוּ (imperative mp); הוֹשֵׁב (absolute); הוֹשִׁיב (construct).

The participle shows מוֹ rather than מַ—for example, מוֹשִׁיבִים—while imperfects show hōlem waw rather than יַ after every preformative consonant—for example, תוֹשַׁבְנָה. Modified forms of the imperfect crop up for jussive (for example, יוֹשֵׁב) and with waw consecutive (וַתּוֹשֶׁב) in Hiphil.

Across its inflection Hophal consistently takes šûreq instead of יַ or יִ, in opening syllables. Perfect favours patah as its second vowel unless volatilized to vocal šᵉwâ.

3ms	הוּשַׁב	3cp	הוּשְׁבוּ
3fs	הוּשְׁבָה		
2ms	הוּשַׁבְתָּ	2mp	הוּשַׁבְתֶּם
2fs	הוּשַׁבְתְּ	2fp	הוּשַׁבְתֶּן
1cs	הוּשַׁבְתִּי	1cp	הוּשַׁבְנוּ

The same is true also for the imperfect (such as נוּשַׁב or יוּשְׁבוּ) and infinitive construct (הוּשַׁב). All second syllables maintain qāmeṣ gādôl in participles except for the alternate feminine singular: that is, מוּשֶׁבֶת.

In the Hiphil (and actually in the Qal too), הלך exhibits features of a pe–waw verb. Accordingly, we encounter Qal imperfect תֵּלְכוּן,

imperative לְכִי and infinitive construct לֶכֶת. Hiphil appears containing ḥōlem waw: הוֹלִיכוֹ or מוֹלִיכֶךָ or יוֹלִיכָהוּ (the illustrations here being displayed with pronominal suffixes).

28.5. *Sibilants within Pe–Waws*

A special category of pe–waw verbs consists of those which have ṣade (or sporadically another sibilant) as their middle root consonant. These verbs conjugate on the analogy of pe–nun verbs. That is, whenever the former waw, now yōd, of a root finds itself at the end of a syllable, the waw/yōd assimilates to the succeeding sibilant letter: תִּיצַת becoming תִּצַּת; אִיצִיעָה becoming אַצִּיעָה; יִיצַג becoming יִצַּג.

There are, however, exceptions whereby the sibilant does not double and the waw/yōd disappears (for example, יִצַק) or becomes part of a vowel (for example, נוֹצַר).

28.6. *Pe–Yōd*

Only seven truly pe–yōd verbs exist in the Hebrew Bible; by happenstance, all are stative in nuance. The Qal stem follows the routine model of strong verbs for perfects, imperatives and infinitives. It is the imperfect Qal that turns aside from that paradigm. In a similar way to the stative verbs of the pe–waw type, the true pe–yōd type retains the yōd (though silent) throughout the imperfect tense. Also like the stative pe–waws, pe–yōds do not retard the tone away from the final syllable after a waw vonsecutive: יִיטְבוּ (3mp imperfect); וַתִּיטַב (3fs or 2ms vav-consecutive imperfect).

Outside of Qal the occurrences of pe–yōd verbs are limited to Piel, Pual and Hiphil. Piel and Pual fit the standard paradigm; Hiphil does not. The latter stem everywhere displaces both יִ and יְ with יֵ: for example, הֵיטַבְתְּ (perfect 2fs); הֵיטִיבָה ('emphatic' imperative ms [Lesson 16.2]); מֵיטִיבֵי (participle mp construct state). Jussives and imperfect consecutives have the forms יֵיטֵב and וַיֵּיטֶב respectively, distinct from the usual imperfect יֵיטִיב which corresponds.

Exercises

Render into English and parse 2 Sam. 12.1-6 according to the previous instructions.

Reading Notes on 2 Samuel 12.1-6

Verse 1:

וַיִּשְׁלַח   Interpret as if spelled וַיִּשְׁלֹח (שלח is lamedh–guttural)

רֹאשׁ   Interpret as if spelled רוֹשׁ (רוש is hollow; ignore the superfluous א)

Verse 3:

קָנָה   Interpret as if spelled קָנָה (קנה is lamedh–he)

וַיְחַיֶּהָ   Interpret as if spelled וַיְחַיְּהֶהָ (חיה is both pe–guttural and lamedh–he)

תִּשְׁתֶּה   Interpret as if spelled תִּשְׁתֶּה (שתה is lamedh–he)

תִּשְׁכָּב   In pause, so that the qāmeṣ is supplanting a pataḥ

וַתְּהִי   Interpret as if spelled וַתְּהִיה

Verse 4:

לַעֲשׂוֹת   Interpret as if spelled לַעֲשׂוֹה

הַבָּא   Interpret as if spelled הַבּוֹא

וַיַּעֲשֶׂהָ   Interpret as if spelled וַיַּעֲשְׂהֶהָ

Verse 5:

וַיִּחַר   Interpret as if spelled וַיִּחְרֹה (חרה is lamedh–he as well as pe–guttural besides ayin–guttural)

הָעֹשֶׂה   Interpret as if spelled הַ0שֶׂה

Verse 6:

עָשָׂה   Interpret as if spelled עָשָׂה

Ayin–Guttural

29.1. Guttural Features

An ayin–guttural verb is one whose middle consonant is a guttural or a resh. The three main features of gutturals and resh (consult Lesson 5.1) all come into play with the inflection of ayin–guttural verbs: gutturals cannot be doubled; gutturals generally take 'a' class vowels (especially pataḥ); and gutturals usually take compound šᵉwâs (especially ḥāṭēp pataḥ).

29.2. Qal

In the perfect tense of Qal the only variation from the standard paradigm is the replacement of ḥāṭēp pataḥ for šᵉwâ in the third feminine singular and third common plural forms: שָׁחֲטָה and שָׁחֲטוּ. Participles exhibit the same composite šᵉwâ outside the masculine singular and alternative feminine singular: for example, שֹׁחֲטִים (mp).

Words with a guttural or resh in the second root position have pataḥ instead of ḥōlem in the second syllable of the imperfect: for example, אֶשְׁחַט. A vocal šᵉwâ, which normally stands in place of such pataḥ beneath the middle root consonant of verb forms having vocalic sufformatives, must become a ḥāṭēp vowel. This includes second feminine singular and both masculine plurals, as well as both cohortatives: for example, תִּשְׁחֲטִי.

The second vowel of Qal imperatives appears also as pataḥ rather than the ḥōlem of strong action verbs. However, when the feminine singular and masculine plural endings are added, the first radical assumes a pataḥ (not a ḥireq [Lesson 16.2]) related to the trailing compound šᵉwâ: for example, שַׁחֲטוּ; שַׁחֲטָנָה.

Qal infinitives behave according to the customary patterns (שְׁחוֹט / שְׁחֹט) except before pronominal suffixes. In these cases the opening sequence of vowels is either ◌ֳ◌ or ◌ַ◌ֲ: for example, שָׁחֲטָם; שָׁחֲטֶךָ.

29.3. *Niphal*

The Niphal of the ayin–guttural is practically normal except that a composite šᵉwâ replaces a simple šᵉwâ under the guttural. This happens with the perfect, imperfect and imperative—as well as with the infinitive construct when it has suffix pronouns: for example, respectively נִשְׁחֲטוּ, תִּשָּׁחֲטִי, הִשָּׁחֲטִי and הִשָּׁחֲטָם.

29.4. *Intensives*

In the so-called intensive stems (Piel, Pual and Hithpael) the ordinary doubling of the second root letter cannot occur. Therefore, intensive stem forms from ayin–guttural verbs are of two kinds, both of which reject dagesh forte:

1. When the middle consonant is aleph or resh the foregoing vowel regularly changes from pataḥ to qāmeṣ gādôl, from ḥireq to ṣērê, or from qibbûṣ to ḥōlem, a trait which is often labelled 'compensatory lengthening'.
2. When the middle consonant is he or heth or even ayin the foregoing vowel usually remains unaltered, a characteristic which is frequently labelled 'virtual (or implicit) doubling'.

In what follows I will employ the paradigmatic verb בָּרַך to illustrate the former category and for the latter, נחם.

In the discussion of the strong verb it was seen that Piel verbs often take a šᵉwâ beneath the middle radical; whenever the second root letter is a guttural, however, this šᵉwâ will become a ḥāṭēp pataḥ. However, as a rule this tends not to take place (but can and sometimes does) where the middle radical is resh.

The following paradigms demonstrate the compensatory lengthening in the root בָּרַך:

Perfect

3ms	בֵּרַך	3cp	בֵּרְכוּ
3fs	בֵּרְכָה		
2ms	בֵּרַכְתָּ	2mp	בֵּרַכְתֶּם
2fs	בֵּרַכְתְּ	2fp	בֵּרַכְתֶּן
1cs	בֵּרַכְתִּי	1cp	בֵּרַכְנוּ

Imperfect

3ms	יְבָרֵךְ	3mp	יְבָרְכוּ
3fs	תְּבָרֵךְ	3fp	תְּבָרֵכְנָה
2ms	תְּבָרֵךְ	2mp	תְּבָרְכוּ
2fs	תְּבָרְכִי	2fp	תְּבָרֵכְנָה
1cs	אֲבָרֵךְ	1cp	נְבָרֵךְ

Imperative

ms	בָּרֵךְ	mp	בָּרְכוּ
fs	בָּרְכִי	fp	בָּרֵכְנָה
Infinitive Construct	בָּרֵךְ	Absolute	בָּרוֹךְ

Participle

ms	מְבָרֵךְ	mp	מְבָרְכִים
fs	מְבָרְכָה / מְבָרֶכֶת	fp	מְבָרְכוֹת

Using the root נחם it is possible to provide illustrations of virtual/implicit doubling: for example, נִחַמְתָּן (perfect); נָחוֹם (infinitive absolute); נְנַחֲמָה (cohortative); מְנַחֵמָה (participle); נַחֵם (imperative).

A waw consecutive on an imperfect of either type detains the accent one place and affects the final vowel: thus, תְּנַחֵם becomes וַתְּנַחֶם.

Pual comparably incorporates either compensatory lengthening before aleph and resh or virtual doubling in he, heth and ayin, and Pual substitutes compound šᵉwâs for simple ones (observing the earlier stipulation regarding resh): for example, נֻחַמְתִּי (perfect); בֹּרְכוּ (perfect); תְּנֻחֲמוּ (imperfect); מְבֹרָכוֹת (participle).

Finally, Hithpael ayin–gutturals observe the same rules: for example, הִתְנַחֲמוּ and הִתְבָּרֵךְ (perfects); אֶתְנַחֵם and יִתְבָּרְכוּ (imperfects); הִתְבָּרֵךְ (infinitive construct); מִתְנַחֵם (participle).

Exercises
Continue with the usual translation and analysis, this time for 1 Kgs 18.41-46.

Reading Notes on 1 Kings 18.41-46

Verse 41:

עָלֹה	Interpret as if spelled עֲלֹה (עלה is lamedh–he besides pe–guttural)
וּשְׁתֵה	Interpret as if spelled וּשְׁתֵה

Verse 42:

וַיַּעֲלֶה	Interpret as if spelled וַיְעֲלֹה
וְלִשְׁתּוֹת	Interpret as if spelled וְלִשְׁתּוֹה
עָלָה	Interpret as if spelled עָלַה
וַיְשֶׂם	Interpret as if spelled וַיְשִׂים (שִׂים is hollow)

Verse 43:

וַיַּעַל	Interpret as if spelled וַיְעֲלֹה
שֵׁב	Interpret as if spelled שׁוּב (שׁוּב is hollow)

Verse 44:

וַיְהִי	Interpret as if spelled וַיִּהְיֶה
עָלָה	Interpret as if spelled עָלְהָ
יַעֲצָרְכָה	כָה is a longer spelling of the suffix pronoun ךָ

Verse 46:

הָיְתָה	Interpret as if spelled הָיְהָה
וַיָּרֶץ	Interpret as if spelled וַיִּרוֹץ (רוּץ is hollow)
בֹּאֲכָה	Interpret as if spelled בּוֹאֲךָ

LESSON 30

Hollow

30.1. *Biliteral Appearance*

The hollow class of weak verbs includes those in which medial waw or medial yōd have lost their consonantal character, having either dropped out of verb forms altogether or else combined with the preceding vowel to yield ḥireq yōd, ḥōlem waw, or šûreq. In all cases, the resultant verb forms are essentially biliteral. Standard Biblical Hebrew dictionaries list the Qal infinitive construct as the root for such terms (for example קוּם) rather than the customary Qal perfect third masculine singular (for example, קָם).

30.2. *Qal Perfect and Active Participle*

Qal perfect action verbs maintain the qāmeṣ of 3ms in 3fs and 3cp; for all other forms the initial vowel is patah:

3ms	קָם	3cp	קָמוּ
3fs	קָמָה		
2ms	קַמְתָּ	2mp	קַמְתֶּם
2fs	קַמְתְּ	2fp	קַמְתֶּן
1cs	קַמְתִּי	1cp	קַמְנוּ

Notice that unlike verbs previously encountered, hollow verbs keep the stress on the initial syllable of 3fs and 3cp.

The sole stative hollow verb with an 'e' class vowel is מוּת. This root follows the action verbs in their use of patah but displays ṣērê where action verbs have qāmeṣ: for example, מֵתוּ, מֵתָה (glance back at Lesson 14.2 for the taw with dagesh forte; the 2ms ending תָּה is a variant of תָּ, with no effect on meaning).

There are several stative verbs displaying 'o' vowels. They are without qāmeṣ gādôl, patah or ṣērê in any first syllable. Instead they carry ḥōlem or ḥōlem waw in all constructions except the second-person plurals, which bear qāmeṣ qāṭān: for example, בֹּשְׁנוּ‎, בָּשְׁתֶּן‎.

The Qal active participle masculine singular is identical with the Qal perfect third masculine singular: for example, קָם. Only the position of its tone on the final syllable distinguishes the feminine singular of the participle (for example, קָמָה) from the third feminine singular of the perfect. The plural participial forms also hold the accent on the last syllable as usual: for example, קָמִים.

30.3. Remaining Qals

While there is no differentiation between hollow verbs with medial waw (so-called ayin–waw roots) and hollow verbs with medial yōd (ayin–yōd roots) in the perfect Qal, there is in the imperfect.

'Ayin waws' contain šûreq or ḥōlem waw in the second syllable.*

3ms	יָקוּם	3mp	יָקוּמוּ
3fs	תָּקוּם	3fp	תְּקוּמֶינָה
2ms	תָּקוּם	2mp	תָּקוּמוּ
2fs	תָּקוּמִי	2fp	תְּקוּמֶינָה
1cs	אָקוּם	1cp	נָקוּם

Ayin–waw verb stative verbs display a replacement of the initial qāmeṣ of the action verb with ṣērê; in addition, a ḥōlem waw replaces šûreq as the second vowel: for example, תֵּבוֹשִׁי.*

'Ayin yōds' contain ḥireq yōd in the second syllable and qāmeṣ in the first.*

3ms	יָבִין	3mp	יָבִינוּ
3fs	תָּבִין	3fp	תְּבִינֶנָה
2ms	תָּבִין	2mp	תָּבִינוּ
2fs	תָּבִינִי	2fp	תְּבִינֶנָה
1cs	אָבִין	1cp	נָבִין

[*A characteristic feature of both ayin–waw and ayin–yōd verbs is that the vocalic sufformatives fail to attract the accent to themselves.]

A linking vowel is commonly omitted before the feminine plural endings of Qal imperfect: thus both תְּקוּמֶינָה and תָּקֹמְנָה are possible, as are תְּבִינֶנָה and תָּבֵנָּה, תֵּבֹשְׁנָה and תְּבוֹשֶׁינָה.

Jussives and waw consecutives of action verbs—but not stative verbs—vary from the full imperfect: for example, imperfect יָקוּם becoming jussive יָקֹם becoming consecutive וַיָּקָם (the last vowel in this last word being qāmeṣ qāṭān) and תָּבִין becoming תָּבֵן becoming וַתָּבֶן.

The imperative also reflects the distinction between verbs displaying middle waw terms and middle yōd verbs, which is what we expect, given how imperatives are formed by eliminating the imperfect pre-formatives of the second person. Qal imperative feminine plurals mimic the imperfect 2fp form that omits any linking vowel: for example, קֹם, בֶּנָה, בּוֹשׁוּ.

Routinely, the infinitive construct of an ayin waw hollow verb matches the imperative masculine singular: for example, קוּם, בֹּשׁ. This is the case for some ayin yōd hollow verbs too: for example, שִׂים. Other ayin yōds however fluctuate in their infinitive construct between the imperative form and a form with šûreq: for example, שִׂים versus שׂוּם.

An infinitive absolute, whether from an action or a stative verb and whether from an ayin–waw or an ayin–yōd root, contains ḥōlem waw or ḥōlem: for example, קוֹם.

Finally, any extant Qal passive participle will look like the infinitive construct.

30.4. *Niphal*

The almost universal occurrence of ḥōlem-waw in the second syllable of the Niphal forms of hollow verbs aids in the recognition of this stem: for example, נָקוֹם (imperfect), הִקּוֹמִי (imperative).*

[*In the derived stems, the contours of 'ayin yōd' and stative 'ayin waw' verbs precisely match those of action 'ayin waw' verbs. Consequently I will employ only קוּם as a model henceforth.]

Several perfects show a šûreq in the first syllable:

3ms	נָקוֹם	3cp	נָקוֹמוּ
3fs	נָקוֹמָה		
2ms	נִקוּמֹוֹתָ	2mp	נִקוּמוֹתֶם
2fs	נִקוּמוֹת	2fp	נִקוּמוֹתֶן
1cs	נִקוּמֹוֹתִי	1cp	נִקוּמֹוֹנוּ

Again a connecting vowel can arise in imperfect 3fp and 2fp: תְּקוֹמֶ֫נָה /
תְּקוֹמֶ֫ינָה.

Context alone determines if הָקֵם is an imperative masculine singular
or an infinitive construct or even an infinitive absolute. Likewise
environment helps to determine whether נָקֵם is perfect 3ms, infinitive
absolute or participle ms. Furthermore, distinguish carefully between
נָקֹ֫מָה (perfect 3fs) and נְקוֹמָה (participle fs).

30.5. *Hiphil and Hophal*

The inflection of the Hiphil perfect exhibits two distinct patterns, one
with a ḥōlem-waw linking vowel (but only in the first and second persons), and one without. Thus it is possible to encounter הֲקֵמְתֶּם (2mp) or
הֲקֵמְתִּי (1cs) or the like. However, the forms with the ḥōlem-waw in a
second syllable are by far more frequent:

3ms	הֵקִים	3cp	הֵקִ֫ימוּ
3fs	הֵקִ֫ימָה		
2ms	הֲקִימֹ֫ותָ	2mp	הֲקִימֹותֶם
2fs	הֲקִימֹות	2fp	הֲקִימֹותֶן
1cs	הֲקִימֹ֫ותִי	1cp	הֲקִימֹ֫ונוּ

The prefix vowel of the perfect and participle 'tenses' is ṣērê while the
other forms have qāmeṣ gādôl.* for example, הָקֵם (infinitive construct). Hiphil imperfects of every hollow verb look exactly like Qal
imperfects of ayin–yōd hollow verb. The same is true for jussives and
cohortatives. Feminine plurals can alternate forms: for example, תָּקֵ֫מִי,
תָּקֵ֫מְנָה / תְּקִימֶ֫ינָה, וַנָּ֫קֶם, יָקֶם

[*Unless of course the vowel is reduced to simple or compound šᵉwâ.]

Throughout the Hophal stem of hollow roots the prefix and preformative vowels are šûreq. Vocalic sufformatives draw the accent to
themselves in Hophal: for example, הוּקְמָ֫נוּ (perfect), תּוּקְמוּ (imperfect),
מוּקֶ֫מֶת (participle).

30.6. *Polel, Polal, Hithpolel*

Apart from a few instances in late Biblical Hebrew, the linguistic
features of which are found in those books composed at a relatively late
date, no Piel, Pual or Hithpael occur for hollow terms. Instead, substitute forms for these three stems were created by means of the repeti-
tion of the final root letter and the insertion of ḥōlem waw after the

initial radical. These forms are designated as *Polel* and *Polal* (in place of Piel and Pual) and *Hithpolel* (for Hithpael). All receive the conventional preformatives and sufformatives. In the perfect, Polel's punctuation matches Polal's except for the 3ms (cf. Lesson 22.5 on Pual matching Piel); the same is also true for several imperfects and participles of Polel and Polal. The following examples help to illustrate:

1. Perfects: קוֹמְמָה (Polel and Polal); קוֹמַמְתֶּם (Polel and Polal); הִתְקוֹמַמְתִּי (Hithpolel)
2. Imperfects: יִתְקוֹמְמוּ (Hithpolel); תְּקוֹמְמִי (Polel and Polal); נְקוֹמַם (Polal)
3. Imperative: הִתְקוֹמֵמְנָה (Hithpolel)
4. Infinitive: קוֹמֵם (Polel)
5. Participle: מְקוֹמָם (Polal)

Exercises
Translate and parse Isa. 49.1-6.

Reading Notes on Isaiah 49.1-6

Verse 1:

קְרָאָנִי   In pause, so that the second qāmeṣ is supplanting a pataḥ

Verse 4:

כִּלֵּיתִי   Interpret as if spelled כִּלֵּהְתִי (כלה is lamedh–he)

Verse 6:

נָקֵל   Interpret as if spelled either נִקְלַל or נְקַלֵל (קלל is geminate)

מִהְיוֹתְךָ   Interpret as if spelled מֵהֱיֹתְךָ

לִהְיוֹת   Iinterpret as if spelled לֶהֱיֹה

Lamedh–Guttural

31.1. *Preference for Pataḥ*

A lamedh–guttural verb has a final radical which is either het, ayin, he + mappîq (הּ)—a combination rarely met in a root consonant. Actually terms ending in aleph or 'plain' he (ה) fit here also but conjugate so differently that they will be treated separately in Lessons 32 and 33. Final resh does not behave as a guttural but as a strong letter.

When dealing with verbs belonging to the lamedh–guttural class, it is perhaps most important to remember that gutturals have a preference for a preceding pataḥ. When a guttural comes at the very end of an inflected form, that pataḥ may be a pataḥ furtive (an element encountered in Lesson 5.1).

31.2. *Qal*

The only form requiring comment in the Qal perfect paradigm is the anomalous שָׁלַחַתְּ (2fs) with an auxiliary pataḥ. It is possible that this unusual spelling was meant by the punctuators to show an option for us to read either שָׁלַחַתְּ—ignoring the dagesh lene and šᵉwâ—or שָׁלַחְתְּ—ignoring the second pataḥ.* It is the latter construction which would have been anticipated since the Qal perfect of lamedh–gutturals is otherwise normal: for example, שָׁלְחָתֶּם.

[*The curious situation arises for the word לקח where the dotted taw distinguishes Qal perfect 2fs, לָקַחַתְּ, from infinitive construct with preposition, לָקַחַת (refer back to Lesson 27.4 for the infinitive).]

Imperfects and imperatives replace any ḥōlem of strong action verbs with a pataḥ, just as strong stative verbs do: for example, נִשְׁלַח, יִשְׁלַח, שְׁלַחְנָה. An imperative bearing the 'paragogic' qāmeṣ + he termination (consult Lesson 16.2) will have ḥireq in the first syllable, again like a stative: thus, שִׁלְחָה. Finally like statives, lamedh–guttural imperfects and imperatives with pronominal suffixes generally take a qāmeṣ Gādôl under the second root letter: for example, שְׁלָחֵנִי, אֶשְׁלָחֲךָ.

The masculine singular forms of the Qal active and passive participles, Qal infinitive absolute and Qal infinitive construct all show the glide vowel furtive pataḥ before a guttural: for example, שֹׁלֵחַ, שָׁלוּחַ, שָׁלֹחַ, שְׁלֹחַ, respectively.

The alternative feminine singular form of the active participle substitutes two pataḥs for two sᵉgōls: that is, שֹׁלַחַת. In other respects lamedh–guttural participles are regular.

With suffixes the infinitive construct can have either qāmeṣ qāṭān or ḥireq in the initial syllable: for example, שָׁלְחִי, שִׁלְחָם.

31.3. *Niphal*

Except for 2fs—נִשְׁלַחַתְּ—Niphal perfect is regular: for example, נִשְׁלְחוּ. So too is its participle, aside from the feminine singular which terminates with taw: נִשְׁלַחַת.

Niphal imperfects and imperatives ending in a guttural manifest pataḥ where strong roots would have ṣērê. This change affects only those verbal shapes which lack sufformatives; the remainder act normally: for example, תִּשָּׁלַח and הִשָּׁלַח (imperfect and imperative lacking sufformatives); תִּשָּׁלַחְנָה and הִשָּׁלְחוּ (possessing sufformatives)

The infinitive construct has the same appearance as the masculine singular imperative. The infinitive absolute, however, differs in form by employing the helping pataḥ: either with the contour of נִשְׁלוֹחַ or of הִשָּׁלֵחַ. The addition of a suffix pronoun to the construct will yield a form such as הִשָּׁלַחֲךָ.

31.4. *Hiphil and Hophal*

Hiphil perfect follows the regular pattern of the strong paradigm, with the exception of the furtive pataḥ in the 3ms and the familiar anomalies of 2fs: that is, הִשְׁלִיחַ, הִשְׁלַחַתְּ.

The Hiphil imperfect without sufformatives take a furtive pataḥ.

3ms	יַשְׁלִיחַ	3mp	יַשְׁלִיחוּ
3fs	תַּשְׁלִיחַ	3fp	תַּשְׁלַחְנָה
2ms	תַּשְׁלִיחַ	2mp	תַּשְׁלִיחוּ
2fs	תַּשְׁלִיחִי	2fp	תַּשְׁלַחְנָה
1cs	אַשְׁלִיחַ	1cp	נַשְׁלִיחַ

From the above it can be seen that the feminine plural imperfects exhibit plain pataḥ rather than ṣērê in the second syllable. The latter feature is true also for jussives and waw consecutives appearing without vocalic sufformatives and for masculine singular and feminine plural imperatives: for example, יִשְׁלַח (jussive), וַנִּשְׁלַח (consecutive), הִשָּׁלַח (imperative).

In contrast, infinitives possess a helper pataḥ, as do the participle's masculine singular: for example, הִשָּׁלֵחַ (absolute), הִשָּׁלִיחַ (construct), מַשְׁלִיחַ (participle). The feminine singular participial variant again has a pair of pataḥs: hence, מַשְׁלַחַת.

The only deviations from strong verbs in the Hophal inflection occur in the perfect 2fs (הָשְׁלַחַתְּ), the participle's feminine singular alternative (מָשְׁלַחַת), and the infinitive absolute (הָשְׁלֵחַ).

31.5. *Piel, Pual, Hithpael*

The full vowel before a lamedh–guttural will be pataḥ as opposed to any ṣērê in the perfect, imperfect, imperative and infinitive construct tenses of the Piel and Hithpael stems. In the perfect 2fs and alternate participle feminine singular there will also be a pataḥ after the guttural. To summarize:

1. Perfects: שִׁלַּחַתְּ (Piel); הִשְׁתַּלַּחְנוּ* (Hithpael)
2. Imperfect: יְשַׁלַּח (Piel)
3. Imperative: הִשְׁתַּלַּחְנָה* (Hithpael)
4. Infinitive Construct or Imperative: שַׁלַּח (Piel)
5. Participle: מִשְׁתַּלַּחַת* (Hithpael)

Pataḥ furtive surfaces in Piel and Hithpael infinitive absolutes—for example, הִשְׁתַּלֵּחַ*—and masculine singular participles—for example, מְשַׁלֵּחַ.

[*For the metathesis of taw and shin see Lesson 24.3.]

Like Hophal, the Pual inflection basically imitates the strong verb. Exceptions here are the now usual 2fs perfect and fs participle: שֻׁלַּחַתְּ, מְשֻׁלַּחַת.

Exercises
Translate Jer. 1.14-19 into English and parse one verb per verse.

Reading Notes on Jeremiah 1.14-19

Verse 16:

וַיִּשְׁתַּחֲווּ   Interpret as if spelled וַיִּשְׁתַּחְוְהוּ (חוה is both pe–guttural
and lamedh–he; see the vocabulary list in Lesson 24)

Verse 17:

אֲצַוְּךָ   Interpret as if spelled אֲצַוְּהֶךָ

תֵּחַת   Interpret as if spelled תֵּחַ1תְּ (חתת is geminate as well as
pe–guttural)

אֲחִתְּךָ   Interpret as if spelled אֲחִתִּיתְךָ

LESSON 32

Lamedh–Aleph

32.1. *Quiescence*

The main feature of a lamedh–aleph root is that the aleph at the end of a syllable loses its power as a consonant, resulting in the syllable becoming, in effect, an open syllable, one concluding with a vowel (recall Lesson 6.2). The aleph is preserved, however, as a fully functioning letter when it stands in front of a vocalic sufformative and thus does not end a syllable. Aleph also avoids quiescence when it begins a syllable—for example, before pronominal suffixes.

32.2. *Qal*

Wherever strong action verbs in Qal perfect have pataḥ, lamedh–aleph action verbs have qāmeṣ. Where strong stative terms show pataḥ, lamedh–aleph statives show ṣērê. Furthermore, no šᵉwâ remains under the aleph in any of those cases, and dagesh lene falls away from the sufformatives which start with taw because the preceding syllable is considered open.

The pattern followed in the action verb is:

3ms	מָצָא	3cp	מָצְאוּ
3fs	מָצְאָה		
2ms	מָצָאתָ	2mp	מְצָאתֶם
2fs	מָצָאת	2fp	מְצָאתֶן
1cs	מָצָאתִי	1cp	מָצָאנוּ

Examples help to illustrate the changes made in the stative verb: מָלֵא rather than מָלַא; מְלֵאתֶם instead of מְלַאתֶם.

Outside the perfect tense both action and stative verbs in the Qal stem follow the same pattern. Imperfect lamedh–alephs replace the ḥōlem or pataḥ of strong verbs with qāmeṣ; with the exception of sᵉgōl in the feminine plurals.

3ms	יִמְצָא	3mp	יִסְצָאוּ
3fs	תִּמְצָא	3fp	תִּמְצֶאנָה
2ms	תִּמְצָא	2mp	תִּמְצָאוּ
2fs	תִּמְצְאִי	2fp	תִּמְצֶאנָה
1cs	אֶמְצָא	1cp	נִמְצָא

When pronouns are suffixed, the imperfect (whether from an action or stative root) of lamedh–aleph takes the form of a strong stative root, which holds qāmeṣ in the second syllable: for example, תִּמְצָאֵהוּ. This tendency was encountered earlier with the larger class of lamedh–gutturals (see Lesson 31).

Since the imperative models itself after the imperfect, an imperative masculine singular likewise has qāmeṣ and feminine plural has sᵉgōl: that is, מְצָא, מְלֶאנָה. Lamedh–aleph participles parallel the lamedh–guttural participles, except for the fact that the feminine singular form which attaches a taw places a ṣērê before the aleph and no vowel behind: that is, מֹצֵאת.

32.3. *Niphal*

The third masculine singular of Niphal perfect appears with qāmeṣ in the final syllable. Elsewhere the pataḥ of strong roots transforms into ṣērê among lamedh–aleph verbs: for example, נִמְצָא, נִמְצֵאתָ, נִמְצֵאתָ.

Like Qal, Niphal imperfect 3fp and 2fp manifest sᵉgōl ahead of the silent aleph (and, naturally, no šᵉwâ beneath it): hence, תִּמָּצֶאנָה. The other contours of Niphal imperfect are normal—adopting the strong inflection: for example, יִמָּצֵא, יִמָּצְאוּ.

According to rule the imperative simply substitutes He for the taw of the matching second-person imperfect, and the only evidence of weakness occurs in the feminine plural: הִמָּצֶאנָה.

Again, as in Qal, Niphal participle feminine singular builds its alternative form with ṣērê: thus, נִמְצֵאת. The rest of the participles are routine, including the feminine singular option נִמְצָאָה.

32.4. *Hiphil and Hophal*

In the Hiphil perfect ṣērê appears in those positions occupied by pataḥ in a strong verb. This vowel change arises when the sufformative starts with a consonant: for example, הִמְצֵאתָ, הִמְצֵאנוּ.

Imperfects show sᵉgōl for ṣērê in the third person and second person feminine plural; imperative follows suit in its feminine plural: תִּמְצֶ֫אנָה and הַמְצֶ֫אנָה.

The Hiphil participle feminine singular with taw added onto a lamedh–aleph term exhibits ṣērê, as do Qal and Niphal: that is, מַמְצֵאת.

In the Hophal inflection the perfect and the imperfect tenses will have qāmeṣ instead of the pataḥ of strong verbs whenever the aleph comes at the end of a word. In some ways this is comparable to Qal. Before a middle-of-the-word aleph, Hophal perfect will have ṣērê instead of pataḥ and Hophal imperfect will have sᵉgōl rather than pataḥ. In this respect Hophal is parallel to Hiphil. Examples help to illustrate the vowel changes: הֻמְצָא, אֻמְצָא, הֻמְצֵ֫אתֶם, תֻּמְצֶ֫אנָה.

The variant Hophal feminine singular participle also imitates the conjugations of other stems: that is, מֻמְצֵאת. It will be observed that Hophal prefixes/preformatives favour qibbûṣ over qāmeṣ qāṭān for lamedh–aleph verbs.

32.5. *Intensives*

In the third masculine singular of Pual perfect, a lamedh–aleph verb will manifest a qāmeṣ gādôl rather than pataḥ in front of the aleph. Elsewhere the perfect tense of all three intensive stems (Piel, Pual and Hithpael) will exhibit ṣērê in place of pataḥ: for example, מֵצָא, מֵצֵ֫אנוּ, הִתְמַצֵּאת, מֵצֵ֫אתֶם.

Throughout the imperfect of Pual the pataḥ vowel is nudged out in favor of a qāmeṣ, except in the 3fp and 2fp where sᵉgōl appears: for example, נְמֻצָּא, תְּמֻצֶּ֫אנָה. Piel and Hithpael imperfect diverge from the strong paradigm only in the feminine plural by assuming sᵉgōl: thus, תִּתְמַצֶּ֫אנָה, תְּמַצֶּ֫אנָה.

Just as for Qal, Niphal and Hiphil, so also Piel and Hithpael imperatives are regular with the exception of the feminine plural: that is, מַצֶּ֫אנָה, הִתְמַצֶּ֫אנָה.

The participles of the intensive stems act analogously to the previous stems by incorporating ṣērê in the final syllable of the feminine singular alternate construction: מְמַצֵּאת, מְמֻצֵּאת, מִתְמַצֵּאת.

Note that the infinitive absolute and infinitive construct are entirely ordinary across the board. Similarly, the Qal passive participle follows the standard strong inflection.

Exercises

Translate and analyze all five verses of Psalm 100.

Reading Notes on Psalm 100

Verse 3:

עָשָׂנוּ   Interpret as if spelled עֲשָׂתָנוּ

Verse 4:

הוֹדוּ   Interpret as if spelled הַיְדִּיהוּ (ידה is lamedh–he in addition to pe–yōd/waw)

LESSON 33

Lamedh–He

33.1. Original Waw

A lamedh–he verb is one whose third radical is a silent he. Most lamedh–he roots were lamedh–yōd at an earlier stage in the development of the language; some were originally lamedh–waw, which turned into lamedh–yōd before lamedh–he. The yōd survives or reappears in several forms of lamedh–he words.

33.2. Qal

In Qal perfect 3ms a qāmeṣ replaces the pataḥ of a strong verb. A taw emerges instead of the radical he in 3fs. The 3cp drops the he and its preceding šᵉwâ from a *theoretical* גָּלְהוּ.

All first and second person forms preserve the original yōd as a silent letter. This letter combines with the vowel ḥireq, which has substituted for the pataḥ of strong roots.

3ms	גָּלָה	3cp	גָּלוּ
3fs	גָּלְתָה		
2ms	גָּלִיתָ	2mp	גְּלִיתֶם
2fs	גָּלִית	2fp	גְּלִיתֶן
1cs	גָּלִיתִי	1cp	גָּלִינוּ

When pronominal suffixes are tacked on to the Qal perfect 3ms, the root consonant he and the vowel in advance of it disappear: for example, גָּלָהוּ (from גָּלָה + הוּ ֡, suffixed pronoun 3ms).

The Qal imperfect without sufformatives will hold a sᵉgōl in the final syllable as opposed to the ḥōlem found in strong verbs. Where vocalic sufformatives are attached to an imperfect, the he of the root along with the hypothetical šᵉwâ which would have preceded falls away. The consonantal sufformative causes the original yōd to reappear; this in turn has a sᵉgōl ahead of it rather than ḥōlem.

3ms	יִגְלֶה	3mp	יִגְלוּ
3fs	תִּגְלֶה	3fp	תִּגְלֶינָה
2ms	תִּגְלֶה	2mp	תִּגְלוּ
2fs	תִּגְלִי	2fp	תִּגְלֶינָה
1cs	אֶגְלֶה	1cp	נִגְלֶה

The radical he and the expected preceding vowel (usually šᵉwâ) are eliminated whenever Qal imperfects receive pronominal suffixes: for example, יִגְלֵם, יִגְלוּךָ.

There are no lamedh–he cohortatives terminating in qāmeṣ + he. Instead the conventional imperfect form is used: thus the form is אֶגְלֶה rather than אֶגְלְהָ or אֶגְלְיָה. The form of the imperfect after waw consecutive and the shape of the jussive appear—in descending order of frequency—as, illustratively, יִגֶל / יֵגֶל / יֶגֶל / יִגְל. Both the singular and plural of the first person assume an abbreviated waw consecutive imperfect construction with these vowels. This phenomenon is attested in no other weak verbs (or strong verb for that matter).

In the Qal imperative masculine singular a ṣērê replaces the sᵉgōl found in the second syllable of the imperfect—after the taw preformative is removed, of course. The feminine singular, masculine plural and feminine plural look exactly like the imperfect minus the taw preformative. In every case a dagesh lene must be inserted into a Begadkefat when it appears as the first letter of the resultant imperative.

ms	גְּלֵה	mp	גְּלוּ
fs	גְּלִי	fp	גְּלֶינָה

The Qal masculine singular active participle ends in ֶה in the absolute state; in the construct state the sᵉgōl + he combination changes to ṣērê + he. Consequently, the construct state of the lamedh–he participle appears identical to the strong verb. For the remainder of the inflection it will be seen that he disappears as do the vowels that would normally precede it. There is, however, a rare feminine singular substitute form which attests a doubled yōd in place of the he. The following examples show the respective changes: גֹּלֶה (absolute ms); גֹּלֵה (construct ms); גֹּלוֹת (fp); גֹּלִיָּה (fs).

Qal passive participles adhere to the strong verbal paradigm except that a yōd takes the place of the third root letter he, as a full consonant: for example, גָּלוּי, גְּלוּים.

In the infinitive construct final he becomes taw. The resultant base of the infinitive construct undergoes no alterations with the addition of a pronominal suffix. The infinitive absolute is completely regular: גָּלֹת, גָּלֹה, גָּלוֹתִי.

33.3. *Niphal*
The inflection of Niphal is quite similar to that of Qal, including (surprisingly) an infinitive construct which concludes with ḥōlem waw and taw: that is, הִגָּלֹת. Niphal differs from Qal in the perfect where ṣērê rather than ḥireq usually arises: for example, נִגְלֵית (2fs). Another distinction can be seen in the jussive and waw consecutive form: that is, יִגָּל.

33.4. *Piel, Pual, Hithpael*
By and large the intensive stems also imitate the Qal conjugation. The exceptions surface (as for Niphal) in the perfect and 'shortened' imperfect tenses. Pual perfect always has ṣērê instead of ḥireq as the vowel of the second syllable. Piel and Hithpael substitute ṣērê merely in the first person singular perfect: for example, הִתְגַּלֵּיתִי, גִּלֵּיתִי, גָּלֵּינוּ.

In Piel and Hithpael the jussive/waw consecutive construction is, for instance, יְגַל and יִתְגַּל respectively.

33.5. *Hiphil and Hophal*
Finally, the causatives (Hiphil and Hophal) copy the Qal model for the most part. Hophal perfect consistently holds ṣērê as opposed to ḥireq, while Hiphil shifts back and forth considerably: for example, הָגְלֵיתָ (2ms, Hophal), הִגְלֵיתֶם / הִגְלִיתֶם (2mp, Hiphil). A further peculiarity of Hiphil is its occasional tendency to change the prefix vowel from ḥireq to sᵉgōl: for example, הֶגְלָה (3ms). Hiphil jussive and imperfect waw consecutive vary little from Qal except that the opening syllable contains sᵉgōl: for example, יֶגֶל.

Exercises
Translate the whole of Psalm 121; then perform parsing on those eight verses.

Reading Notes on Psalm 121

Verse 3:

לַמּוֹט   Interpret as if spelled לָמוּט (in the tense at hand of hollow action verbs we sometimes find ḥōlem waw or ḥōlem for the more usual šûreq)

LESSON 34

Geminate

34.1. *Consonant Duplication*

Geminate verbs (often called double ayin or ayin–ayin verbs) are those whose second root consonant has been duplicated. Dictionaries will list such terms with all three letters—for example, סָבַב. However, the majority of inflectional forms will collapse the final two radicals into a doubled letter or even a single letter: for example, הֵסוֹב, מְסִבָּה.

34.2. *Qal*

Action verbs in Qal perfect will normally produce third person forms containing both of the root's duplicated consonants. Furthermore, 3fs and 3cp may have either the simple vocal šᵉwâ or ḥāṭēp pataḥ under the middle radical. In all other conjugations of the perfect tense the final two (identical) letters merge into one; this consonant then takes a dagesh forte and is followed by the connecting vowel, ḥōlem-waw.

3ms	סָבַב	3cp	סָבְבוּ / סָבֲבוּ
3fs	סָבְבָה / סָבֲבָה		
2ms	סַבּוֹתָ	2mp	סַבּוֹתֶם
2fs	סַבּוֹת	2fp	סַבּוֹתֶן
1cs	סַבּוֹתִי	1cp	סַבּוֹנוּ

Qal perfect statives double the coalesced second/third consonant everywhere other than 3ms, which has the root letter written only once and undoubled: for example, תַּם, תַּמּוֹתִי, תַּמּוּ, תַּמּוֹתֶן. (Observe the presence of the ḥōlem-waw link.)

The imperfect continues to distinguish between action and stative verbs. Additionally, it divides each of these categories into two kinds. The second kind consistently introduces dagesh forte into the initial radical and tends to remove any doubling dot from the subsequent letter. The first kind does not make such changes. Thus verbs of the first kind with their slightly biconsonantal appearance resemble Ayin waw hollow roots while verbs of the second kind with the doubling of their initial radical are analogous to pe–nun roots. The following summary might help to clarify:

Type 1. Action verbs manifest qāmeṣ under the preformative (except šᵉwâ in the feminine plurals), ḥōlem as the second vowel (but qibbûṣ in feminine plural), and a doubled consonant before sufformatives (along with a sᵉgōl + yōd linking vowel in 3fp and 2fp): for example, תָּסֹב, תָּסֹבְּינָה, תָּסֹבּוּ. Stative words place ṣērê beneath preformatives (except 3fp/2fp) and pataḥ as the next vowel: for example, יֵתַם, תֵּתַמִּי, תִּתְמֶינָה.

 An imperfect construction is attested for action verbs of the first type when attached to waw consecutive: for example, וַיָּסָב. (The third vowel is qāmeṣ qāṭān.)

Type 2. Action roots have ḥireq in the preformative syllable (but sᵉgōl in 1cs), followed by a doubled consonant which in turn is followed by a ḥōlem (but šᵉwâ in 2fs/3mp/2mp); there is no dagesh in the final visible radical: for example, תִּסֹב, אֶסֹב, תִּסֹּבְנָה, יִסֹּבוּ. Statives likewise show preformatives with ḥireq (apart from 1cs) succeeded by a letter with dagesh; however, the second syllable has pataḥ and the duplicated root consonant generally remains doubled in front of vocalic sufformatives: for example, יִתַּם, אֶתַּם, תִּתַּמְנָה, תִּתַּמּוּ.

Qal imperatives simulate the first kind of imperfect, for both the verbs of action:

| | ms | סֹב | mp | סֹבּוּ |
| | fs | סֹבִּי | fp | סֻבֶּינָה |

and stative verbs:

| | ms | תַּם | mp | תַּמּוּ |
| | fs | תַּמִּי | fp | תַּמֶּינָה |

The infinitive construct of an action verb oscillates between a contour like the imperative masculine singular and a contour incorporating the last two radicals written individually; the stative infinitive construct always looks like the imperative of a verb of action: that is, סֹב, סְבֹב (this item mimics the strong paradigm), תַּם.

Both active and passive participles as well as infinitive absolutes are regular in appearance. Thus, the participle appears as, for example, סֹבֵב, סְבוּבִים; the infinitive as תָּמוֹם, סָבוֹב.

34.3. *Niphal*

The initial vowel of the Niphal perfect is qāmeṣ gādôl in the third person and šᵉwâ in the first and second person conjugations. The next vowel is pataḥ throughout. The first and second person forms show a syllable with ḥōlem-waw before suffformatives. Only 3ms fails to double the merged final pair of radicals. Curiously, 3ms produces a few instances in which ṣērê appears abnormally in the second syllable, similar to stative verbs in Qal perfect: for example, נָסַב and נָסֵב (3ms), נָסַבָּה (3fs), נְסַבּוֹתֶם (2mp).

A masculine singular participle differs from a 3ms perfect in having a qāmeṣ in the final syllable. (Here too, however, an anomalous ṣērê can arise.) Every other form has pataḥ as the second vowel. The feminine singular participle differs from 3fs perfect by shifting the accent to the final syllable and by reducing the vowel at the beginning: for example, נְסַבָּה, נְסַבַּת, נָסֵב, נָסָב.

In Niphal imperfect, imperative, and infinitives the first root letter is doubled across the board. So too is the second/third root letter when succeeded by a suffformative. The former results from assimilation of the stem prefix nun, while the latter arises from the coalescence of the identical geminate consonants. With one exception (the 3fp/2fp form), Niphal imperfects share the same shape as the second type of Qal stative imperfects (discussed in the second section of the present lesson). He merely replaces taw to transform an imperfect into an imperative: for example, יִסַּבּוּ (3mp), תִּסַּבֶּינָה (3fp/2fp), נִסַּב (1cp), הִסַּב (ms), הִסַּבִּי (fs).

The closing vowel for the infinitive absolute is ḥōlem-waw and ṣērê for infinitive construct: that is, הִסּוֹב, הִסֵּב.

34.4. *Causatives*

Ṣērê is the prefix vowel in the perfect and participle of Hiphil. This vowel reduces to ḥāṭēp pataḥ for all forms of the perfect which add consonantal suffformatives and to šᵉwâ in all participial forms which accept any format ending. The vowel of the second syllable is a ṣērê in third person perfects* and masculine singular participles but ḥireq else-where. Notice that a connecting vowel appears in most perfect forms and a doubled letter arises before each sufformative/inflectional ending. It is helpful to present all the forms:

Perfect:

3ms	הֵסֵב	3cp	הֵסֵבּוּ
3fs	הֵסֵבָּה		
2ms	הֲסִבּוֹתָ	2mp	הֲסִבּוֹתֶם
2fs	הֲסִבּוֹת	2fp	הֲסִבּוֹתֶן
1cs	הֲסִבּוֹתִי	1cp	הֲסִבּוֹנוּ

Participle:

ms	מֵסֵב	mp	מְסִבִּים
fs	מְסִבָּה	fp	מְסִבּוֹת

[*Some verbs, especially Qal statives, may include pataḥ in the second syllable of Hiphil perfect 3ms and 3cp: for example, הֵסַב, הֵסַבּוּ.]

Hiphil imperfect verbs can, like Qal, be divided into two types: those with and those without dagesh in the initial radical. In those appearing without dagesh forte, the first root letter is preceded by qāmeṣ and fol-lowed by ṣērê (unless šᵉwâ and ḥireq, in a feminine plural). In those verbs with dagesh, the first root letter follows pataḥ but precedes ṣērê, even in 3fp/2fp.

Verbs of the first type follow the pattern: אָסֵב, תְּסֻבֶּינָה. The form of the second type is: תָּסֵב, יָסֵבּוּ. Again, as in Qal, the imperfect of the for-mer type have a shortened waw consecutive shape (וַיָּסֶב). All impera-tives adhere to the rules governing the first type (הָסֵב, הָסֵבּוּ). Both infinitives, absolute and construct, adopt the masculine singular im-perative style: that is, הָסֵב.

The prefix vowel in every Hophal is šûreq, apart from the second type of imperfect which possesses qibbûṣ. Qāmeṣ crops up in the participle's second syllable; other tenses take pataḥ. As in the foregoing derived stems, in Hophal the geminate root consonants fuse into a doubled or single letter and are not written separately: for example, הוּסַבָּה (per-fect); יוּסַבּוּ and יֻסַב (imperfects); מוּסָב (participle). (Parallels to pe–yōd/waw and hollow terms will be observed.)

34.5. *Piel, Pual, Hithpael*

Piel, Pual and Hithpael either conjugate as if strong verbs or inflect along the lines of hollow intensives (compare Lesson 30.6). These latter inflections are known as Poel, Poal and Hithpoel. A few examples help to illustrate:

1. Poel: תְּסוֹבֵבְנָה (imperfect) סוֹבֵב (perfect, imperative or infinitive)
2. Poal: יְסוֹבַב (imperfect) מְסוֹבָב (participle)
3. Hithpoel: הִסְתּוֹבַבְתְּ (perfect) הִסְתּוֹבֵבוּ (perfect or imperative)

Exercises

Analyze Prov. 3.13-18 after you have rendered it into English.

APPENDIX

Alternative Schemes for Vowel Sounds

ַ , pataḥ and ָ , qāmeṣ (gādôl)	= *u* as in 'cup'
ֶ , sᵉgōl and ֵ , ṣērê and ֵי , ṣērê yōd	= *e* as in 'pen'
ִ , ḥireq and ִי , ḥireq yōd	= *i* as in 'big'
ָ , qāmeṣ qāṭān and ֹ , ḥōlem and וֹ, ḥōlem waw	= *o* as in 'strong'
ֻ , qibbûṣ and וּ, šûreq	= *u* as in 'put'

ַ , pataḥ	= *a* as in 'pat'
ָ , qāmeṣ (gādôl) and ָ , qāmeṣ qāṭān	= *o* as in 'strong'
ֶ , sᵉgōl	= *e* as in 'pen'
ֵ , ṣērê and ֵי , ṣērê yōd	= *e* as in 'they'
ִ , ḥireq and ִי , ḥireq yōd	= *i* as in 'machine'
ֹ ḥōlem and וֹ, ḥōlem waw	= *o* as in 'bone'
ֻ , qibbûṣ and וּ, šûreq	= *u* as in 'put'

ַ , pataḥ	= *a* as in 'pat'
ֶ , sᵉgōl	= *e* as in 'pen'
ִ , ḥireq	= *i* as in 'big'
ָ , qāmeṣ qāṭān	= *o* as in 'strong'
ֻ , qibbûṣ	= *u* as in 'put'
ָ , qāmeṣ (gādôl)	= *a* as in 'raj'
ֵ , ṣērê and ֵי , ṣērê yōd	= *e* as in 'they'
ִי , ḥireq yōd	= *i* as in 'machine'
ֹ ḥōlem and וֹ, ḥōlem waw	= *o* as in 'bone'
וּ, šûreq	= *u* as in 'flute'

VOCABULARY

אָב	father	אֶרֶץ	earth, land
אָבַד	to perish	אֵשׁ	fire
אֶבֶן	stone	אִשָּׁה	woman, wife
אַבְרָם / אַבְרָהָם	Abraham/Abram	אֲשֶׁר	who, which, that
אָדוֹן	lord, master	אַתְּ	you (fs)
אָדָם	human beings	אֵת	(direct object marker)
אֲדָמָה	ground		
אָהַב	to love	אֵת	with
אֹהֶל	tent	אַתָּה	you (ms)
אַהֲרֹן	Aaron	אַתֶּם	you (mp)
אוֹ	or	אַתֵּן / אַתֵּנָה	you (fp)
אֹזֶן	ear		
אָח	brother	בְּ	in, by
אֶחָד	one	בָּבֶל	Babylon
אַחֲרֵי / אַחַר	after	בֶּגֶד	garment
אֹיֵב	enemy	בְּהֵמָה	animal
אַיִן	nothing	בּוֹא	to come, enter
אִישׁ	man, husband	בָּחַר	to choose
אָכַל	to eat	בֵּין	between
אַל	not	בַּיִת	house
אֶל	toward	בֵּן	son
אֵל	God	בָּנָה	to build
אֵלֶּה	these	בִּנְיָמִן	Benjamin
אֱלֹהִים	God, gods	בַּעַל	lord, husband
אֶלֶף	thousand	בָּקָר	cattle
אֵם	mother	בֹּקֶר	morning
אִם	if	בָּקַשׁ	to seek
אַמָּה	cubit	בְּרִית	covenant
אָמַר	to say	בָּרַךְ	to bless
אֲנַחְנוּ	we	בָּשָׂר	flesh
אָנֹכִי / אֲנִי	I	בַּת	daughter
אָסַף	to gather		
אַף	nose; anger	גְּבוּל	border
אֶפְרַיִם	Ephraim	גָּדוֹל	great
אַרְבַּע	four	גּוֹי	nation
אֲרוֹן	ark	גָּלָה	to uncover, reveal

גַּם	also, even	יָדַע	to know
		יְהוּדָה	Judah
דָּבַר	to speak	יהוה	Yahweh
דָּבָר	word, thing	יְהוֹשֻׁעַ	Joshua
דָּוִד	David	יוֹם	day
דָּם	blood	יוֹסֵף	Joseph
דֶּרֶךְ	way	יָכֹל	to be able
		יָלַד	to bear, beget
הַ	the	יָם	sea
הֲ	(interrogative particle)	יָסַף	to add
הוּא	that (m); he, it	יַעֲקֹב	Jacob
הִיא	that (f); she, it	יָצָא	to go out/forth
הָיָה	to be, happen	יָרֵא	to fear
הָלַךְ	to go, walk	יָרַד	to go down
הֵמָּה / הֵם	they, those (m)	יַרְדֵּן	Jordan
הֵנָּה	they, those (f)	יְרוּשָׁלַיִם	Jerusalem
הִנֵּה	behold, lo	יָרַשׁ	to inherit
הַר	mountain	יִשְׂרָאֵל	Israel
		יָשַׁב	to sit, dwell
וְ	and	יָשַׁע	to save
זֹאת	this (f)	כְּ	like, as
זֶה	this (m)	כָּבוֹד	glory, honor
זָהָב	gold	כֹּה	so, thus
זָכַר	to remember	כֹּהֵן	priest
זָקֵן	old	כּוּן	to be firm or established
זֶרַע	seed, offspring	כִּי	because, that, when, indeed
חֹדֶשׁ	month, new moon	כֹּל	all, every
חָוָה	to bow down	כָּלָה	to be finished
חָזַק	to be(come) strong	כְּלִי	vessel
חָטָא	to sin	כֵּן	so, thus
חַטָּאת	sin	כֶּסֶף	money, silver
חַי	alive	כַּף	palm; sole
חָיָה	to live	כָּרַת	to cut
חַיִל	strength, army	כָּתַב	to write
חָמֵשׁ	five		
חֶסֶד	kindness	לְ	to, for
חָצֵר	settlement, court	לֹא	not
חֶרֶב	sword	לֵב (or לֵבָב)	heart
		לֵוִי	Levi, Levite
טוֹב	good	לָחַם	to fight
		לֶחֶם	bread, food
יָד	hand	לַיְלָה	night

לָכֵן	therefore	נָצַל	to deliver
לְמַעַן	for the sake of	נָשָׂא	to lift, carry
לִפְנֵי	before	נָתַן	to give, allow, put
לָקַח	to take		
		סָבִיב	around
מְאֹד	very	סוּר	to turn aside
מֵאָה	hundred	סֵפֶר	book
מִדְבָּר	wilderness		
מָה	what	עָבַד	to serve
מוֹאָב	Moab	עֶבֶד	servant
מוֹעֵד	appointed place or time	עָבַר	to pass over
		עַד	until
מוּת	to die	עוֹד	again, still
מִזְבֵּחַ	altar	עוֹלָם	eternity
מַחֲנֶה	camp	עָוֹן	iniquity
מַטֶּה	rod; tribe	עָזַב	to leave
מִי	who	עַיִן	eye, fountain
מַיִם	water	עִיר	city
מָלֵא	to be full	עַל	upon
מַלְאָךְ	messenger, angel	עָלָה	to go up
מִלְחָמָה	war, battle	עֹלָה	burnt offering
מָלַךְ	to reign	עַם	people
מֶלֶךְ	king	עִם	with
מִן	from	עָמַד	to stand
מִנְחָה	gift, offering	עָנָה	to answer
מַעֲשֶׂה	work	עֵץ	tree, wood
מָצָא	to find	עָשָׂה	to do, make
מִצְוָה	commandment	עֶשֶׂר	ten
מִצְרַיִם	Egypt	עֵת	time
מָקוֹם	place	עַתָּה	now
מֹשֶׁה	Moses		
מִשְׁפָּחָה	clan	פֶּה	mouth
מִשְׁפָּט	judgment	פְּלִשְׁתִּי	Philistine
		פָּנִים	face
נָא	please	פָּקַד	to appoint; visit
נְאֻם	utterance	פַּרְעֹה	Pharaoh
נָבִיא	prophet		
נָגַד	to tell	צֹאן	flock (of sheep or goats)
נַחֲלָה	possession		
נָטָה	to turn aside; extend	צָבָא	army
		צַדִּיק	righteous
נָכָה	to smite	צִוָּה	to command
נַעַר	lad		
נָפַל	to fall	קָדַשׁ	to be holy
נֶפֶשׁ	soul, person	קֹדֶשׁ	holiness

קוֹל	voice, sound	שֵׁבֶט	rod; tribe
קוּם	to rise, stand	שָׁבַע	to swear
קָרָא	to call, read	שֶׁבַע	seven
קָרַב	to draw near	שׁוּב	to turn, return
קֶרֶב	midst	שָׁכַב	to lie down
		שָׁלוֹם	peace
רָאָה	to see	שָׁלַח	to send
רֹאשׁ	head	שְׁלֹמֹה	Solomon
רַב	much, numerous	שָׁלֹשׁ	three
רָבָה	to be(come)	שָׁם	there
	numerous	שֵׁם	name
רֶגֶל	foot	שָׁמַיִם	heaven(s)
רוּחַ	spirit, wind	שֶׁמֶן	oil
רוּם	to be high	שְׁמֹנֶה	eight
רַע	bad	שָׁמַע	to hear
רֵעַ	friend	שָׁמַר	to guard, observe
רָעָה	to tend (flocks)	שָׁנָה	year
רָעָה	wickedness	שְׁנַיִם	two
רָשָׁע	guilty	שַׁעַר	gate
		שָׁפַט	to judge
שָׂדֶה	field	שֵׁשׁ	six
שִׂים	to place	שָׁתָה	to drink
שָׂפָה	lip		
שַׂר	leader, official	תָּוֶךְ	midst
		תּוֹרָה	law
שָׁאוּל	Saul	תַּחַת	under
שָׁאַל	to ask	תֵּשַׁע	nine

PARADIGM 1
Strong Verb

	Qal		Niphal	Piel
Perfect				
3ms	קָטַל	שָׁכֵל	נִקְטַל	קִטֵּל
3fs	קָטְלָה	שָׁכְלָה	נִקְטְלָה	קִטְּלָה
2ms	קָטַ֫לְתָּ	שָׁכַ֫לְתָּ	נִקְטַ֫לְתָּ	קִטַּ֫לְתָּ
2fs	קָטַלְתְּ	שָׁכַלְתְּ	נִקְטַלְתְּ	קִטַּלְתְּ
1cs	קָטַ֫לְתִּי	שָׁכַ֫לְתִּי	נִקְטַ֫לְתִּי	קִטַּ֫לְתִּי
3cp	קָטְלוּ	שָׁכְלוּ	נִקְטְלוּ	קִטְּלוּ
2mp	קְטַלְתֶּם	שְׁכַלְתֶּם	נִקְטַלְתֶּם	קִטַּלְתֶּם
2fp	קְטַלְתֶּן	שְׁכַלְתֶּן	נִקְטַלְתֶּן	קִטַּלְתֶּן
1cp	קָטַ֫לְנוּ	שָׁכַ֫לְנוּ	נִקְטַ֫לְנוּ	קִטַּ֫לְנוּ
Imperfect				
3ms	יִקְטֹל	יִשְׁכַּל	יִקָּטֵל	יְקַטֵּל
3fs	תִּקְטֹל	תִּשְׁכַּל	תִּקָּטֵל	תְּקַטֵּל
2ms	תִּקְטֹל	תִּשְׁכַּל	תִּקָּטֵל	תְּקַטֵּל
2fs	תִּקְטְלִי	תִּשְׁכְּלִי	תִּקָּטְלִי	תְּקַטְּלִי
1cs	אֶקְטֹל	אֶשְׁכַּל	אֶקָּטֵל	אֲקַטֵּל
3mp	יִקְטְלוּ	יִשְׁכְּלוּ	יִקָּטְלוּ	יְקַטְּלוּ
3fp	תִּקְטֹלְנָה	תִּשְׁכַּלְנָה	תִּקָּטֵלְנָה	תְּקַטֵּלְנָה
2mp	תִּקְטְלוּ	תִּשְׁכְּלוּ	תִּקָּטְלוּ	תְּקַטְּלוּ
2fp	תִּקְטֹלְנָה	תִּשְׁכַּלְנָה	תִּקָּטֵלְנָה	תְּקַטֵּלְנָה
1cp	נִקְטֹל	נִשְׁכַּל	נִקָּטֵל	נְקַטֵּל
Imperative				
ms	קְטֹל	שְׁכַל	הִקָּטֵל	קַטֵּל
fs	קִטְלִי	שִׁכְלִי	הִקָּטְלִי	קַטְּלִי
mp	קִטְלוּ	שִׁכְלוּ	הִקָּטְלוּ	קַטְּלוּ
fp	קְטֹלְנָה	שְׁכַלְנָה	הִקָּטֵלְנָה	קַטֵּלְנָה
Infinitive				
cstr.	קְטֹל		הִקָּטֵל	קַטֵּל
abs.	קָטוֹל		הִקָּטֹל and נִקְטֹל	קַטֵּל
Participle				
ms	קָטוּל / קֹטֵל		נִקְטָל	מְקַטֵּל
	(active)/(passive)	—		

	Pual	Hiphil	Hophal	Hithpael
Perfect				
3ms	קֻטַּל	הִקְטִיל	הָקְטַל	הִתְקַטֵּל
3fs	קֻטְּלָה	הִקְטִֿילָה	הָקְטְלָה	הִתְקַטְּלָה
2ms	קֻטַּֿלְתָּ	הִקְטַֿלְתָּ	הָקְטַֿלְתָּ	הִתְקַטַּֿלְתָּ
2fs	קֻטַּלְתְּ	הִקְטַלְתְּ	הָקְטַלְתְּ	הִתְקַטַּלְתְּ
1cs	קֻטַּֿלְתִּי	הִקְטַֿלְתִּי	הָקְטַֿלְתִּי	הִתְקַטַּֿלְתִּי
3cp	קֻטְּלוּ	הִקְטִֿילוּ	הָקְטְלוּ	הִתְקַטְּלוּ
2mp	קֻטַּלְתֶּם	הִקְטַלְתֶּם	הָקְטַלְתֶּם	הִתְקַטַּלְתֶּם
2fp	קֻטַּלְתֶּן	הִקְטַלְתֶּן	הָקְטַלְתֶּן	הִתְקַטַּלְתֶּן
1cp	קֻטַּֿלְנוּ	הִקְטַֿלְנוּ	הָקְטַֿלְנוּ	הִתְקַטַּֿלְנוּ
Imperfect				
3ms	יְקֻטַּל	יַקְטִיל	יָקְטַל	יִתְקַטֵּל
3fs	תְּקֻטַּל	תַּקְטִיל	תָּקְטַל	תִּתְקַטֵּל
2ms	תְּקֻטַּל	תַּקְטִיל	תָּקְטַל	תִּתְקַטֵּל
2fs	תְּקֻטְּלִי	תַּקְטִֿילִי	תָּקְטְלִי	תִּתְקַטְּלִי
1cs	אֲקֻטַּל	אַקְטִיל	אָקְטַל	אֶתְקַטֵּל
3mp	יְקֻטְּלוּ	יַקְטִֿילוּ	יָקְטְלוּ	יִתְקַטְּלוּ
3fp	תְּקֻטַּֿלְנָה	תַּקְטֵֿלְנָה	תָּקְטַֿלְנָה	תִּתְקַטֵּֿלְנָה
2mp	תְּקֻטְּלוּ	תַּקְטִֿילוּ	תָּקְטְלוּ	תִּתְקַטְּלוּ
2fp	תְּקֻטַּֿלְנָה	תַּקְטֵֿלְנָה	תָּקְטַֿלְנָה	תִּתְקַטֵּֿלְנָה
1cp	נְקֻטַּל	נַקְטִיל	נָקְטַל	נִתְקַטֵּל
Imperative				
ms	—	הַקְטֵל	—	הִתְקַטֵּל
fs	—	הַקְטִֿילִי	—	הִתְקַטְּלִי
mp	—	הַקְטִֿילוּ	—	הִתְקַטְּלוּ
fp	—	הַקְטֵֿלְנָה	—	הִתְקַטֵּֿלְנָה
Infinitive				
cstr.	wanting	הַקְטִיל	wanting	הִתְקַטֵּל
abs.	קֻטֹּל	הַקְטֵל	הָקְטֵל	הִתְקַטֵּל
Participle				
ms	מְקֻטָּל	מַקְטִיל	מָקְטָל	מִתְקַטֵּל

Note that with the exception of 3 masculine singular, E-class stative verbs (such as כָּבֵד) conjugate in the perfect exactly like action verbs (represented here by קָטַל). In the imperfect, imperative and infinitive, E-class statives inflect the same way as O-class statives (represented by שָׁכֹל).

PARADIGM 2
Strong Verb in Qal with Suffixes

	1cs (נִ)	2ms (ךָ)	2fs (ךְ)	3ms (וֹ / הוּ)
Perfect				
3ms	קְטָלַנִי	קְטָלְךָ	קְטָלֵךְ	קְטָלוֹ
3fs	קְטָלַתְנִי	קְטָלַתְךָ	קְטָלַתֶךְ	קְטָלַתּוּ / קְטָלַתְהוּ
2ms	קְטַלְתַּנִי	—	—	קְטַלְתּוֹ
2fs/1cs	קְטַלְתִּינִי	קְטַלְתִּיךָ	קְטַלְתִּיךְ	קְטַלְתִּיו / קְטַלְתִּיהוּ
3cp	קְטָלוּנִי	קְטָלוּךָ	קְטָלוּךְ	קְטָלוּהוּ
2mp/2fp	קְטַלְתּוּנִי	—	—	קְטַלְתּוּהוּ
1cp	—	קְטַלְנוּךָ	קְטַלְנוּךְ	קְטַלְנוּהוּ
Imperfect				
3ms	יִקְטְלֵנִי	יִקְטָלְךָ	יִקְטְלֵךְ	יִקְטְלֵהוּ

(The 3ms row on both pages is a guide for all imperfects ending in consonants.)

3mp	יִקְטְלוּנִי	יִקְטְלוּךָ	יִקְטְלוּךְ	יִקְטְלוּהוּ

(The 3mp row is a guide for imperfects ending in vowels.)

Imperative				
ms	קָטְלֵנִי	—	—	קָטְלֵהוּ
mp	קִטְלוּנִי	—	—	קִטְלוּהוּ

(This mp row across both sheets is a template for the feminines too.)

Infinitive				
	קָטְלִי / קָטְלֵנִי	קָטְלְךָ	קָטְלֵךְ	קָטְלוֹ

	3fs (הָ / ה)	1cp (נוּ)	2mp (כֶם)	3mp (ם)	3fp (ן)
Perfect					
3ms	קְטָלָהּ	קְטָלָנוּ	wanting	קְטָלָם	קְטָלָן
3fs	קְטָלַתָּה	קְטָלַתְנוּ	wanting	קְטָלָתַם	wanting
2ms	קְטַלְתָּהּ	קְטַלְתָּנוּ	—	קְטַלְתָּם	wanting
2fs/1cs	קְטַלְתִּיהָ	קְטַלְתִּינוּ	wanting	קְטַלְתִּים	קְטַלְתִּין
3cp	קְטָלוּהָ	קְטָלוּנוּ	wanting	קְטָלוּם	קְטָלוּן
2mp/2fp	wanting	קְטַלְתּוּנוּ	—	wanting	wanting
1cp	קְטַלְנוּהָ	—	קְטַלְנוּכֶם	קְטַלְנוּם	wanting
Imperfect					
3ms	יִקְטְלָהּ / יִקְטְלֶהָ	יִקְטְלֵנוּ	יִקְטָלְכֶם	יִקְטְלֵם	wanting
3mp	יִקְטְלוּהָ	יִקְטְלוּנוּ	יִקְטְלוּכֶם	יִקְטְלוּם	יִקְטְלוּן
Imperative					
ms	קְטָלָהּ / קְטָלֶהָ	קְטָלֵנוּ	—	קְטָלֵם	wanting
mp	קְטָלוּהָ	קְטָלוּנוּ	—	קְטָלוּם	wanting
Infinitive					
	קְטָלָהּ	קְטָלֵנוּ	קְטָלְכֶם	קְטָלָם	קְטָלָן

Note that for stative verbs in the perfect tense with suffixed pronouns, a ṣērê substitutes for the first qāmeṣ of 3ms, 3fs and 3cp action verbs (for example, לְבֵשֵׁנִי in place of קְטָלָנִי). In stative imperfects, the second šᵉwâ of action verbs becomes a qāmeṣ gādôl (for example, יִלְבָּשׁוּנִי rather than יִקְטְלוּנִי). There are, however, exceptions to this rule: qāmeṣ replaces a qāmeṣ qāṭān in the 3ms imperfect model before a 2ms suffix (יִלְבָּשְׁךָ for יִקְטָלְךָ), while a qāmeṣ qāṭān ahead of a 2mp suffix alters to pataḥ (יִלְבַּשְׁכֶם for יִקְטָלְכֶם).

PARADIGM 3
Pe–Guttural Verb

	Qal		Niphal
Perfect			
3ms	עָמַד		נֶעֱמַד
3fs	עָמְדָה		נֶעֶמְדָה
2ms	עָמַׂדְתָּ		נֶעֱמַׂדְתָּ
2fs	עָמַדְתְּ		נֶעֱמַדְתְּ
1cs	עָמַׂדְתִּי		נֶעֱמַׂדְתִּי
3cp	עָמְדוּ		נֶעֶמְדוּ
2mp	עֲמַדְתֶּם		נֶעֱמַדְתֶּם
2fp	עֲמַדְתֶּן		נֶעֱמַדְתֶּן
1cp	עָמַׂדְנוּ		נֶעֱמַׂדְנוּ
Imperfect			
3ms	יַעֲמֹד	יֶחֱזַק	יֵעָמֵד
3fs	תַּעֲמֹד	תֶּחֱזַק	תֵּעָמֵד
2ms	תַּעֲמֹד	תֶּחֱזַק	תֵּעָמֵד
2fs	תַּעַמְדִי	תֶּחֶזְקִי	תֵּעָמְדִי
1cs	אֶעֱמֹד	אֶחֱזַק	אֵעָמֵד
3mp	יַעַמְדוּ	יֶחֶזְקוּ	יֵעָמְדוּ
3fp	תַּעֲמֹׂדְנָה	תֶּחֱזַׂקְנָה	תֵּעָמַׂדְנָה
2mp	תַּעַמְדוּ	תֶּחֶזְקוּ	תֵּעָמְדוּ
2fp	תַּעֲמֹׂדְנָה	תֶּחֱזַׂקְנָה	תֵּעָמַׂדְנָה
1cp	נַעֲמֹד	נֶחֱזַק	נֵעָמֵד
Imperative			
ms	עֲמֹד	חֲזַק	הֵעָמֵד
fs	עִמְדִי	חִזְקִי	הֵעָמְדִי
mp	עִמְדוּ	חִזְקוּ	הֵעָמְדוּ
fp	עֲמֹׂדְנָה	הֲזַׂקְנָה	הֵעָמַׂדְנָה
Infinitive			
cstr.		עֲמֹד	הֵעָמֵד
abs.		עָמוֹד	הֵעָמוֹד and נַעֲמוֹד
Participle			
ms	עָמוּד / עֹמֵד	—	נֶעֱמָד
	(active)/(passive)		

	Hiphil	Hophal
Perfect		
3ms	הֶעֱמִיד	הָעֳמַד
3fs	הֶעֱמִידָה	הָעָמְדָה
2ms	הֶעֱמַדְתָּ	הָעֳמַדְתָּ
2fs	הֶעֱמַדְתְּ	הָעֳמַדְתְּ
1cs	הֶעֱמַדְתִּי	הָעֳמַדְתִּי
3cp	הֶעֱמִידוּ	הָעָמְדוּ
2mp	הֶעֱמַדְתֶּם	הָעֳמַדְתֶּם
2fp	הֶעֱמַדְתֶּן	הָעֳמַדְתֶּן
1cp	הֶעֱמַדְנוּ	הָעֳמַדְנוּ
Imperfect		
3ms	יַעֲמִיד	יָעֳמַד
3fs	תַּעֲמִיד	תָּעֳמַד
2ms	תַּעֲמִיד	תָּעֳמַד
2fs	תַּעֲמִידִי	תָּעֳמְדִי
1cs	אַעֲמִיד	אָעֳמַד
3mp	יַעֲמִידוּ	יָעֳמְדוּ
3fp	תַּעֲמֵדְנָה	תָּעֳמַדְנָה
2mp	תַּעֲמִידוּ	תָּעֳמְדוּ
2fp	תַּעֲמֵדְנָה	תָּעֳמַדְנָה
1cp	נַעֲמִיד	נָעֳמַד
Imperative		
ms	הַעֲמֵד	—
fs	הַעֲמִידִי	—
mp	הַעֲמִידוּ	—
fp	הַעֲמֵדְנָה	—
Infinitive		
cstr.	הַעֲמִיד	wanting
abs.	הַעֲמֵד	הָעֳמֵד
Participle		
ms	מַעֲמִיד	מָעֳמָד

PARADIGM 4
Pe–Aleph Verb

	Qal	
Perfect		
3ms	אָכַל	
3fs	אָכְלָה	
2ms	אָכַלְתָּ	
2fs	אָכַלְתְּ	
1cs	אָכַלְתִּי	
3cp	אָכְלוּ	
2mp	אֲכַלְתֶּם	
2fp	אֲכַלְתֶּן	
1cp	אָכַלְנוּ	
Imperfect		
3ms	יֹאכַל	יֶאֱזֹר
3fs	תֹּאכַל	תֶּאֱזֹר
2ms	תֹּאכַל	תֶּאֱזֹר
2fs	תֹּאכְלִי	תַּאַזְרִי
1cs	אֹכַל	אֶאֱזֹר
3mp	יֹאכְלוּ	יַאַזְרוּ
3fp	תֹּאכַלְנָה	תֶּאֱזֹרְנָה
2mp	תֹּאכְלוּ	תַּאַזְרוּ
2fp	תֹּאכַלְנָה	תֶּאֱזֹרְנָה
1cp	נֹאכַל	נֶאֱזֹר
Imperative		
ms	אֱכֹל	
fs	אִכְלִי	
mp	אִכְלוּ	
fp	אֱכֹלְנָה	
Infinitive		
cstr.	אֱכֹל	
abs.	אָכוֹל	
Participle		
ms	אָכוּל/אֹכֵל	
	(active)/(passive)	

PARADIGM 5
Pe–Waw Verb

	Qal		Niphal
Perfect			
3ms	יָשַׁב		נוֹשַׁב
3fs	יָשְׁבָה		נוֹשְׁבָה
2ms	יָשַׁבְתָּ		נוֹשַׁבְתָּ
2fs	יָשַׁבְתְּ		נוֹשַׁבְתְּ
1cs	יָשַׁבְתִּי		נוֹשַׁבְתִּי
3cp	יָשְׁבוּ		נוֹשְׁבוּ
2mp	יְשַׁבְתֶּם		נוֹשַׁבְתֶּם
2fp	יְשַׁבְתֶּן		נוֹשַׁבְתֶּן
1cp	יָשַׁבְנוּ		נוֹשַׁבְנוּ
Imperfect			
3ms	יֵשֵׁב	יִירַשׁ	יִוָּשֵׁב
3fs	תֵּשֵׁב	תִּירַשׁ	תִּוָּשֵׁב
2ms	תֵּשֵׁב	תִּירַשׁ	תִּוָּשֵׁב
2fs	תֵּשְׁבִי	תִּירְשִׁי	תִּוָּשְׁבִי
1cs	אֵשֵׁב	אִירַשׁ	אִוָּשֵׁב
3mp	יֵשְׁבוּ	יִירְשׁוּ	יִוָּשְׁבוּ
3fp	תֵּשַׁבְנָה	תִּירַשְׁנָה	תִּוָּשַׁבְנָה
2mp	תֵּשְׁבוּ	תִּירְשׁוּ	תִּוָּשְׁבוּ
2fp	תֵּשַׁבְנָה	תִּירַשְׁנָה	תִּוָּשַׁבְנָה
1cp	נֵשֵׁב	נִירַשׁ	נִוָּשֵׁב
Imperative			
ms	שֵׁב	רַשׁ	הִוָּשֵׁב
fs	שְׁבִי	רְשִׁי	הִוָּשְׁבִי
mp	שְׁבוּ	רְשׁוּ	הִוָּשְׁבוּ
fp	שֵׁבְנָה	רַשְׁנָה	הִוָּשַׁבְנָה
Infinitive			
cstr.	שֶׁבֶת		הִוָּשֵׁב
abs.	יָשׁוֹב		הִוָּשֵׁב
Participle			
ms	יָשׁוּב / יֵשֵׁב	—	נוֹשָׁב
	(active)/(passive)		

	Hiphil	Hophal
Perfect		
3ms	הוֹשִׁיב	הוּשַׁב
3fs	הוֹשִׁיבָה	הוּשְׁבָה
2ms	הוֹשַׁבְתָּ	הוּשַׁבְתָּ
2fs	הוֹשַׁבְתְּ	הוּשַׁבְתְּ
1cs	הוֹשַׁבְתִּי	הוּשַׁבְתִּי
3cp	הוֹשִׁיבוּ	הוּשְׁבוּ
2mp	הוֹשַׁבְתֶּם	הוּשַׁבְתֶּם
2fp	הוֹשַׁבְתֶּן	הוּשַׁבְתֶּן
1cp	הוֹשַׁבְנוּ	הוּשַׁבְנוּ
Imperfect		
3ms	יוֹשִׁיב	יוּשַׁב
3fs	תּוֹשִׁיב	תּוּשַׁב
2ms	תּוֹשִׁיב	תּוּשַׁב
2fs	תּוֹשִׁיבִי	תּוּשְׁבִי
1cs	אוֹשִׁיב	**א**וּשַׁב
3mp	יוֹשִׁיבוּ	יוּשְׁבוּ
3fp	תּוֹשֵׁבְנָה	תּוּשַׁבְנָה
2mp	תּוֹשִׁיבוּ	תּוּשְׁבוּ
2fp	תּוֹשֵׁבְנָה	תּוּשַׁבְנָה
1cp	נוֹשִׁיב	נוּשַׁב
Imperative		
ms	הוֹשֵׁב	—
fs	הוֹשִׁיבִי	—
mp	הוֹשִׁיבוּ	—
fp	הוֹשֵׁבְנָה	—
Infinitive		
cstr.	הוֹשִׁיב	הוּשַׁב
abs.	הוֹשֵׁב	הוּשֵׁב
Participle	מוֹשִׁיב	
ms		מוּשָׁב

PARADIGM 6
Pe–Yōd Verb

	Qal	Hiphil
Perfect		
3ms	יָטֵב	הֵיטִיב
3fs	יָטְבָה	הֵיטִיבָה
2ms	יָטַבְתָּ	הֵיטַבְתָּ
2fs	יָטַבְתְּ	הֵיטַבְתְּ
1cs	יָטַבְתִּי	הֵיטַבְתִּי
3cp	יָטְבוּ	הֵיטִיבוּ
2mp	יְטַבְתֶּם	הֵיטַבְתֶּם
2fp	יְטַבְתֶּן	הֵיטַבְתֶּן
1cp	יָטַבְנוּ	הֵיטַבְנוּ
Imperfect		
3ms	יִיטַב	יֵיטִיב
3fs	תִּיטַב	תֵּיטִיב
2ms	תִּיטַב	תֵּיטִיב
2fs	תִּיטְבִי	תֵּיטִיבִי
1cs	אִיטַב	אֵיטִיב
3mp	יִיטְבוּ	יֵיטִיבוּ
3fp	תִּיטַבְנָה	תֵּיטֵבְנָה
2mp	תִּיטְבוּ	תֵּיטִיבוּ
2fp	תִּיטַבְנָה	תֵּיטֵבְנָה
1cp	נִיטַב	נֵיטִיב
Imperative		
ms	wanting	הֵיטֵב
fs	wanting	הֵיטִיבִי
mp	wanting	הֵיטִיבוּ
fp	wanting	הֵיטֵבְנָה
Infinitive		
cstr.	יְטֹב	הֵיטִיב
abs.	יָטוֹב	הֵיטֵב
Participle		
ms	—	מֵיטִיב

PARADIGM 7
Pe–Nun Verb

	Qal		Niphal	Hiphil	Hophal
Perfect					
3ms		נָפַל	נִגַּשׁ	הִגִּישׁ	הֻגַּשׁ
3fs		נָפְלָה	נִגְּשָׁה	הִגִּישָׁה	הֻגְּשָׁה
2ms		נָפַֽלְתָּ	נִגַּֽשְׁתָּ	הִגַּֽשְׁתָּ	הֻגַּֽשְׁתָּ
2fs		נָפַלְתְּ	נִגַּשְׁתְּ	הִגַּשְׁתְּ	הֻגַּשְׁתְּ
1cs		נָפַֽלְתִּי	נִגַּֽשְׁתִּי	הִגַּֽשְׁתִּי	הֻגַּֽשְׁתִּי
3cp		נָפְלוּ	נִגְּשׁוּ	הִגִּישׁוּ	הֻגְּשׁוּ
2mp		נְפַלְתֶּם	נִגַּשְׁתֶּם	הִגַּשְׁתֶּם	הֻגַּשְׁתֶּם
2fp		נְפַלְתֶּן	נִגַּשְׁתֶּן	הִגַּשְׁתֶּן	הֻגַּשְׁתֶּן
1cp		נָפַֽלְנוּ	נִגַּֽשְׁנוּ	הִגַּֽשְׁנוּ	הֻגַּֽשְׁנוּ
Imperfect					
3ms	יִפֹּל	יִגַּשׁ	יִנָּגֵשׁ	יַגִּישׁ	יֻגַּשׁ
3fs	תִּפֹּל	תִּגַּשׁ	תִּנָּגֵשׁ	תַּגִּישׁ	תֻּגַּשׁ
2ms	תִּפֹּל	תִּגַּשׁ	תִּנָּגֵשׁ	תַּגִּישׁ	תֻּגַּשׁ
2fs	תִּפְּלִי	תִּגְּשִׁי	תִּנָּגְשִׁי	תַּגִּֽישִׁי	תֻּגְּשִׁי
1cs	אֶפֹּל	אֶגַּשׁ	אֶנָּגֵשׁ	אַגִּישׁ	אֻגַּשׁ
3mp	יִפְּלוּ	יִגְּשׁוּ	יִנָּגְשׁוּ	יַגִּֽישׁוּ	יֻגְּשׁוּ
3fp	תִּפֹּֽלְנָה	תִּגַּֽשְׁנָה	תִּנָּגַֽשְׁנָה	תַּגֵּֽשְׁנָה	תֻּגַּֽשְׁנָה
2mp	תִּפְּלוּ	תִּגְּשׁוּ	תִּנָּגְשׁוּ	תַּגִּֽישׁוּ	תֻּגְּשׁוּ
2fp	תִּפֹּֽלְנָה	תִּגַּֽשְׁנָה	תִּנָּגַֽשְׁנָה	תַּגֵּֽשְׁנָה	תֻּגַּֽשְׁנָה
1cp	נִפֹּל	נִגַּשׁ	נִנָּגֵשׁ	נַגִּישׁ	נֻגַּשׁ
Imperative					
ms	נְפֹל	גַּשׁ	הִנָּגֵשׁ	הַגֵּשׁ	—
fs	נִפְלִי	גְּשִׁי	הִנָּגְשִׁי	הַגִּֽישִׁי	—
mp	נִפְלוּ	גְּשׁוּ	הִנָּגְשׁוּ	הַגִּֽישׁוּ	—
fp	נְפֹֽלְנָה	גַּֽשְׁנָה	הִנָּגַֽשְׁנָה	הַגֵּֽשְׁנָה	—
Infinitive					
cstr.	נְפֹל	גֶּֽשֶׁת	הִנָּגֵשׁ	הַגִּישׁ	הֻגַּשׁ
abs.		נָפוֹל	נִגּוֹשׁ	הַגֵּשׁ	הֻגֵּשׁ
Participle					
ms	נֹפֵל / נָפוּל		—	נִגָּשׁ	מַגִּישׁ	מֻגָּשׁ
	(active/passive)				

PARADIGM 8
Ayin–Guttural Verb

	Qal	Niphal	Piel	Pual	Hithpael
Perfect					
3ms	שָׁחַט	נִשְׁחַט	בֵּרַךְ	בֹּרַךְ	הִתְבָּרֵךְ
3fs	שָׁחֲטָה	נִשְׁחֲטָה	בֵּרְכָה	בֹּרְכָה	הִתְבָּרְכָה
2ms	שָׁחַ֫טְתָּ	נִשְׁחַ֫טְתָּ	בֵּרַ֫כְתָּ	בֹּרַ֫כְתָּ	הִתְבָּרַ֫כְתָּ
2fs	שָׁחַטְתְּ	נִשְׁחַטְתְּ	בֵּרַכְתְּ	בֹּרַכְתְּ	הִתְבָּרַכְתְּ
1cs	שָׁחַ֫טְתִּי	נִשְׁחַ֫טְתִּי	בֵּרַ֫כְתִּי	בֹּרַ֫כְתִּי	הִתְבָּרַ֫כְתִּי
3cp	שָׁחֲטוּ	נִשְׁחֲטוּ	בֵּרְכוּ	בֹּרְכוּ	הִתְבָּרְכוּ
2mp	שְׁחַטְתֶּם	נִשְׁחַטְתֶּם	בֵּרַכְתֶּם	בֹּרַכְתֶּם	הִתְבָּרַכְתֶּם
2fp	שְׁחַטְתֶּן	נִשְׁחַטְתֶּן	בֵּרַכְתֶּן	בֹּרַכְתֶּן	הִתְבָּרַכְתֶּן
1cp	שָׁחַ֫טְנוּ	נִשְׁחַ֫טְנוּ	בֵּרַ֫כְנוּ	בֹּרַ֫כְנוּ	הִתְבָּרַ֫כְנוּ
Imperfect					
3ms	יִשְׁחַט	יִשָּׁחֵט	יְבָרֵךְ	יְבֹרַךְ	יִתְבָּרֵךְ
3fs	תִּשְׁחַט	תִּשָּׁחֵט	תְּבָרֵךְ	תְּבֹרַךְ	תִּתְבָּרֵךְ
2ms	תִּשְׁחַט	תִּשָּׁחֵט	תְּבָרֵךְ	תְּבֹרַךְ	תִּתְבָּרֵךְ
2fs	תִּשְׁחֲטִי	תִּשָּׁחֲטִי	תְּבָרְכִי	תְּבֹרְכִי	תִּתְבָּרְכִי
1cs	אֶשְׁחַט	אֶשָּׁחֵט	אֲבָרֵךְ	אֲבֹרַךְ	אֶתְבָּרֵךְ
3mp	יִשְׁחֲטוּ	יִשָּׁחֲטוּ	יְבָרְכוּ	יְבֹרְכוּ	יִתְבָּרְכוּ
3fp	תִּשְׁחַ֫טְנָה	תִּשָּׁחַ֫טְנָה	תְּבָרֵ֫כְנָה	תְּבֹרַ֫כְנָה	תִּתְבָּרֵ֫כְנָה
2mp	תִּשְׁחֲטוּ	תִּשָּׁחֲטוּ	תְּבָרְכוּ	תְּבֹרְכוּ	תִּתְבָּרְכוּ
2fp	תִּשְׁחַ֫טְנָה	תִּשָּׁחַ֫טְנָה	תְּבָרֵ֫כְנָה	תְּבֹרַ֫כְנָה	תִּתְבָּרֵ֫כְנָה
1cp	נִשְׁחַט	נִשָּׁחֵט	נְבָרֵךְ	נְבֹרַךְ	נִתְבָּרֵךְ
Imperative					
ms	שְׁחַט	הִשָּׁחֵט	בָּרֵךְ	—	הִתְבָּרֵךְ
fs	שַׁחֲטִי	הִשָּׁחֲטִי	בָּרְכִי	—	הִתְבָּרְכִי
mp	שַׁחֲטוּ	הִשָּׁחֲטוּ	בָּרְכוּ	—	הִתְבָּרְכוּ
fp	שְׁחַ֫טְנָה	הִשָּׁחַ֫טְנָה	בָּרֵ֫כְנָה	—	הִתְבָּרֵ֫כְנָה
Infinitive					
cstr.	שְׁחֹט	הִשָּׁחֵט	בָּרֵךְ	wanting	הִתְבָּרֵךְ
abs.	שָׁחוֹט	נִשְׁחוֹט	בָּרוֹךְ	wanting	הִתְבָּרֵךְ
Participle					
ms	שָׁחוּט / שֹׁחֵט (active/passive)	נִשְׁחָט	מְבָרֵךְ	מְבֹרָךְ	מִתְבָּרֵךְ

PARADIGM 9
Hollow Verb

	Qal		Niphal	Polel
Perfect				
3ms	קָם	בּוֹשׁ	נָקוֹם	קוֹמֵם
3fs	קָמָה	בּוֹשָׁה	נָקוֹמָה	קוֹמְמָה
2ms	קַמְתָּ	בֹּשְׁתָּ	נְקוּמֹוֹתָ	קוֹמַמְתָּ
2fs	קַמְתְּ	בֹּשְׁתְּ	נְקוּמוֹת	קוֹמַמְתְּ
1cs	קַמְתִּי	בֹּשְׁתִּי	נְקוּמֹוֹתִי	קוֹמַמְתִּי
3cp	קָמוּ	בּוֹשׁוּ	נָקוֹמוּ	קוֹמְמוּ
2mp	קַמְתֶּם	בָּשְׁתֶּם	נְקוֹמוֹתֶם	קוֹמַמְתֶּם
2fp	קַמְתֶּן	בָּשְׁתֶּן	נְקוֹמוֹתֶן	קוֹמַמְתֶּן
1cp	קַמְנוּ	בֹּשְׁנוּ	נְקוּמֹוֹנוּ	קוֹמַמְנוּ
Imperfect				
3ms	יָקוּם	יֵבוֹשׁ	יִקּוֹם	יְקוֹמֵם
3fs	תָּקוּם	תֵּבוֹשׁ	תִּקּוֹם	תְּקוֹמֵם
2ms	תָּקוּם	תֵּבוֹשׁ	תִּקּוֹם	תְּקוֹמֵם
2fs	תָּקוּמִי	תֵּבוֹשִׁי	תִּקּוֹמִי	תְּקוֹמְמִי
1cs	אָקוּם	אֵבוֹשׁ	אֶקּוֹם	אֲקוֹמֵם
3mp	יָקוּמוּ	יֵבוֹשׁוּ	יִקּוֹמוּ	יְקוֹמְמוּ
3fp	תְּקוּמֶינָה	תֵּבוֹשֶׁינָה	תִּקּוֹמֶינָה	תְּקוֹמֵמְנָה
2mp	תָּקוּמוּ	תֵּבוֹשׁוּ	תִּקּוֹמוּ	תְּקוֹמְמוּ
2fp	תְּקוּמֶינָה	תֵּבוֹשֶׁינָה	תִּקּוֹמֶינָה	תְּקוֹמֵמְנָה
1cp	נָקוּם	נֵבוֹשׁ	נִקּוֹם	נְקוֹמֵם
Imperative				
ms	קוּם	בּוֹשׁ	הִקּוֹם	קוֹמֵם
fs	קוּמִי	בּוֹשִׁי	הִקּוֹמִי	קוֹמְמִי
mp	קוּמוּ	בּוֹשׁוּ	הִקּוֹמוּ	קוֹמְמוּ
fp	קֹמְנָה	בֹּשְׁנָה	הִקּוֹמְנָה	קוֹמֵמְנָה
Infinitive				
cstr.	קוּם	בּוֹשׁ	הִקּוֹם	קוֹמֵם
abs.	קוֹם	בּוֹשׁ	הִקּוֹם and נָקוֹם	קוֹמֵם
Participle				
ms	קוּם / קָם	—	נָקוֹם	מְקוֹמֵם
	(active)/(passive)			

	Polal	Hiphil	Hophal	Hithpolel
Perfect				
3ms	קוֹמַם	הֵקִים	הוּקַם	הִתְקוֹמֵם
3fs	קוֹמְמָה	הֵקִימָה	הוּקְמָה	הִתְקוֹמְמָה
2ms	קוֹמַׂמְתָּ	הֲקִימֹוֹתָ	הוּקַׂמְתָּ	הִתְקוֹמַׂמְתָּ
2fs	קוֹמַמְתְּ	הֲקִימוֹת	הוּקַמְתְּ	הִתְקוֹמַמְתְּ
1cs	קוֹמַׂמְתִּי	הֲקִימֹוֹתִי	הוּקַׂמְתִּי	הִתְקוֹמַׂמְתִּי
3cp	קוֹמְמוּ	הֵקִׂימוּ	הוּקְמוּ	הִתְקוֹמְמוּ
2mp	קוֹמַמְתֶּם	הֲקִימוֹתֶם	הוּקַמְתֶּם	הִתְקוֹמַמְתֶּם
2fp	קוֹמַׂמְתֶּן	הֲקִימוֹתֶן	הוּקַמְתֶּן	הִתְקוֹמַׂמְתֶּן
1cp	קוֹמַׂמְנוּ	הֲקִימֹוֹנוּ	הוּקַׂמְנוּ	הִתְקוֹמַׂמְנוּ
Imperfect				
3ms	יְקוֹמַם	יָקִים	יוּקַם	יִתְקוֹמֵם
3fs	תְּקוֹמַם	תָּקִים	תּוּקַם	תִּתְקוֹמֵם
2ms	תְּקוֹמַם	תָּקִים	תּוּקַם	תִּתְקוֹמֵם
2fs	תְּקוֹמְמִי	תָּקִׂימִי	תּוּקְמִי	תִּתְקוֹמְמִי
1cs	אֲקוֹמַם	אָקִים	אוּקַם	אֶתְקוֹמֵם
3mp	יְקוֹמְמוּ	יָקִׂימוּ	יוּקְמוּ	יִתְקוֹמְמוּ
3fp	תְּקוֹמַׂמְנָה	תְּקִימֶׂינָה	תּוּקַׂמְנָה	תִּתְקוֹמַׂמְנָה
2mp	תְּקוֹמְמוּ	תָּקִׂימוּ	תּוּקְמוּ	תִּתְקוֹמְמוּ
2fp	תְּקוֹמַׂמְנָה	תְּקִימֶׂינָה	תּוּקַׂמְנָה	תִּתְקוֹמַׂמְנָה
1cp	נְקוֹמַם	נָקִים	נוּקַם	נִתְקוֹמֵם
Imperative				
ms	—	הָקֵם	—	הִתְקוֹמֵם
fs	—	הָקִׂימִי	—	הִתְקוֹמְמִי
mp	—	הָקִׂימוּ	—	הִתְקוֹמְמוּ
fp	—	הָקֵׂמְנָה	—	הִתְקוֹמַׂמְנָה
Infinitive				
cstr.	wanting	הָקִים	הוּקַם	הִתְקוֹמֵם
abs.	wanting	הָקֵם	הוּקֵם	הִתְקוֹמֵם
Participle				
ms	מְקוֹמָם	מֵקִים	מוּקָם	מִתְקוֹמֵם

Note that the imperfect, imperative, infinitive construct and passive participle tenses in the Qal stem of ayin–yōd roots depart from the pattern of action ayin–waws (see קוּם above). Middle yōd Qal imperfects imitate middle waw Hiphil imperfects. Qal imperatives of medial yōds are בִּין, בִּינִי, בִּינוּ and בִּנָה. Qal infinitive constructs and passive participles usually equal the masculine singular imperative.

PARADIGM 10
Lamedh–Guttural Verb

	Qal	Niphal	Piel	Pual
Perfect				
3ms	שָׁלַח	נִשְׁלַח	שִׁלַּח	שֻׁלַּח
3fs	שָׁלְחָה	נִשְׁלְחָה	שִׁלְּחָה	שֻׁלְּחָה
2ms	שָׁלַחְתָּ	נִשְׁלַחְתָּ	שִׁלַּחְתָּ	שֻׁלַּחְתָּ
2fs	שָׁלַחַתְּ	נִשְׁלַחַתְּ	שִׁלַּחַתְּ	שֻׁלַּחַתְּ
1cs	שָׁלַחְתִּי	נִשְׁלַחְתִּי	שִׁלַּחְתִּי	שֻׁלַּחְתִּי
3cp	שָׁלְחוּ	נִשְׁלְחוּ	שִׁלְּחוּ	שֻׁלְּחוּ
2mp	שְׁלַחְתֶּם	נִשְׁלַחְתֶּם	שִׁלַּחְתֶּם	שֻׁלַּחְתֶּם
2fp	שְׁלַחְתֶּן	נִשְׁלַחְתֶּן	שִׁלַּחְתֶּן	שֻׁלַּחְתֶּן
1cp	שָׁלַחְנוּ	נִשְׁלַחְנוּ	שִׁלַּחְנוּ	שֻׁלַּחְנוּ
Imperfect				
3ms	יִשְׁלַח	יִשָּׁלַח	יְשַׁלַּח	יְשֻׁלַּח
3fs	תִּשְׁלַח	תִּשָּׁלַח	תְּשַׁלַּח	תְּשֻׁלַּח
2ms	תִּשְׁלַח	תִּשָּׁלַח	תְּשַׁלַּח	תְּשֻׁלַּח
2fs	תִּשְׁלְחִי	תִּשָּׁלְחִי	תְּשַׁלְּחִי	תְּשֻׁלְּחִי
1cs	אֶשְׁלַח	אֶשָּׁלַח	אֲשַׁלַּח	אֲשֻׁלַּח
3mp	יִשְׁלְחוּ	יִשָּׁלְחוּ	יְשַׁלְּחוּ	יְשֻׁלְּחוּ
3fp	תִּשְׁלַחְנָה	תִּשָּׁלַחְנָה	תְּשַׁלַּחְנָה	תְּשֻׁלַּחְנָה
2mp	תִּשְׁלְחוּ	תִּשָּׁלְחוּ	תְּשַׁלְּחוּ	תְּשֻׁלְּחוּ
2fp	תִּשְׁלַחְנָה	תִּשָּׁלַחְנָה	תְּשַׁלַּחְנָה	תְּשֻׁלַּחְנָה
1cp	נִשְׁלַח	נִשָּׁלַח	נְשַׁלַּח	נְשֻׁלַּח
Imperative				
ms	שְׁלַח	הִשָּׁלַח	שַׁלַּח	—
fs	שִׁלְחִי	הִשָּׁלְחִי	שַׁלְּחִי	—
mp	שִׁלְחוּ	הִשָּׁלְחוּ	שַׁלְּחוּ	—
fp	שְׁלַחְנָה	הִשָּׁלַחְנָה	שַׁלַּחְנָה	—
Infinitive				
cstr.	שְׁלֹחַ	הִשָּׁלַח	שַׁלַּח	wanting
abs.	שָׁלוֹחַ	הִשָּׁלֵחַ and נִשְׁלוֹחַ	שַׁלֵּחַ	wanting
Participle				
ms	שָׁלוּחַ / שֹׁלֵחַ	נִשְׁלָח	מְשַׁלֵּחַ	מְשֻׁלָּח
	(active)/(passive)			

	Hiphil	Hophal	Hithpael
Perfect			
3ms	הִשְׁלִיחַ	הָשְׁלַח	הִשְׁתַּלַּח
3fs	הִשְׁלִיחָה	הָשְׁלְחָה	הִשְׁתַּלְּחָה
2ms	הִשְׁלַ֫חְתָּ	הָשְׁלַ֫חְתָּ	הִשְׁתַּלַּ֫חְתָּ
2fs	הִשְׁלַחַתְּ	הָשְׁלַחַתְּ	הִשְׁתַּלַּחַתְּ
1cs	הִשְׁלַ֫חְתִּי	הָשְׁלַ֫חְתִּי	הִשְׁתַּלַּ֫חְתִּי
3cp	הִשְׁלִיחוּ	הָשְׁלְחוּ	הִשְׁתַּלְּחוּ
2mp	הִשְׁלַחְתֶּם	הָשְׁלַחְתֶּם	הִשְׁתַּלַּחְתֶּם
2fp	הִשְׁלַחְתֶּן	הָשְׁלַחְתֶּן	הִשְׁתַּלַּחְתֶּן
1cp	הִשְׁלַ֫חְנוּ	הָשְׁלַ֫חְנוּ	הִשְׁתַּלַּ֫חְנוּ
Imperfect			
3ms	יַשְׁלִיחַ	יָשְׁלַח	יִשְׁתַּלַּח
3fs	תַּשְׁלִיחַ	תָּשְׁלַח	תִּשְׁתַּלַּח
2ms	תַּשְׁלִיחַ	תָּשְׁלַח	תִּשְׁתַּלַּח
2fs	תַּשְׁלִ֫יחִי	תָּשְׁלְחִי	תִּשְׁתַּלְּחִי
1cs	אַשְׁלִיחַ	אָשְׁלַח	אֶשְׁתַּלַּח
3mp	יַשְׁלִ֫יחוּ	יָשְׁלְחוּ	יִשְׁתַּלְּחוּ
3fp	תַּשְׁלַ֫חְנָה	תָּשְׁלַ֫חְנָה	תִּשְׁתַּלַּ֫חְנָה
2mp	תַּשְׁלִ֫יחוּ	תָּשְׁלְחוּ	תִּשְׁתַּלְּחוּ
2fp	תַּשְׁלַ֫חְנָה	תָּשְׁלַ֫חְנָה	תִּשְׁתַּלַּ֫חְנָה
1cp	נַשְׁלִיחַ	נָשְׁלַח	נִשְׁתַּלַּח
Imperative			
ms	הַשְׁלַח	—	הִשְׁתַּלַּח
fs	הַשְׁלִ֫יחִי	—	הִשְׁתַּלְּחִי
mp	הַשְׁלִ֫יחוּ	—	הִשְׁתַּלְּחוּ
fp	הַשְׁלַ֫חְנָה	—	הִשְׁתַּלַּ֫חְנָה
Infinitive			
cstr.	הַשְׁלִיחַ	wanting	הִשְׁתַּלַּח
abs.	הַשְׁלֵחַ	הָשְׁלֵחַ	הִשְׁתַּלֵּחַ
Participle			
ms	מַשְׁלִיחַ	מָשְׁלָח	מִשְׁתַּלֵּחַ

PARADIGM 11
Lamedh–Aleph Verb

	Qal		Niphal	Piel
Perfect				
3ms	מָצָא	מָלֵא	נִמְצָא	מִצֵּא
3fs	מָצְאָה	מָלְאָה	נִמְצְאָה	מִצְּאָה
2ms	מָצָאתָ	מָלֵאתָ	נִמְצֵאתָ	מִצֵּאתָ
2fs	מָצָאת	מָלֵאת	נִמְצֵאת	מִצֵּאת
1cs	מָצָאתִי	מָלֵאתִי	נִמְצֵאתִי	מִצֵּאתִי
3cp	מָצְאוּ	מָלְאוּ	נִמְצְאוּ	מִצְּאוּ
2mp	מְצָאתֶם	מְלֵאתֶם	נִמְצֵאתֶם	מִצֵּאתֶם
2fp	מְצָאתֶן	מְלֵאתֶן	נִמְצֵאתֶן	מִצֵּאתֶן
1cp	מָצָאנוּ	מָלֵאנוּ	נִמְצֵאנוּ	מִצֵּאנוּ
Imperfect				
3ms	יִמְצָא		יִמָּצֵא	יְמַצֵּא
3fs	תִּמְצָא		תִּמָּצֵא	תְּמַצֵּא
2ms	תִּמְצָא		תִּמָּצֵא	תְּמַצֵּא
2fs	תִּמְצְאִי		תִּמָּצְאִי	תְּמַצְּאִי
1cs	אֶמְצָא		אֶמָּצֵא	אֲמַצֵּא
3mp	יִמְצְאוּ		יִמָּצְאוּ	יְמַצְּאוּ
3fp	תִּמְצֶאנָה		תִּמָּצֶאנָה	תְּמַצֶּאנָה
2mp	תִּמְצְאוּ		תִּמָּצְאוּ	תְּמַצְּאוּ
2fp	תִּמְצֶאנָה		תִּמָּצֶאנָה	תְּמַצֶּאנָה
1cp	נִמְצָא		נִמָּצֵא	נְמַצֵּא
Imperative				
ms	מְצָא		הִמָּצֵא	מַצֵּא
fs	מִצְאִי		הִמָּצְאִי	מַצְּאִי
mp	מִצְאוּ		הִמָּצְאוּ	מַצְּאוּ
fp	מְצֶאנָה		הִמָּצֶאנָה	מַצֶּאנָה
Infinitive				
cstr.	מְצֹא		הִמָּצֵא	מַצֵּא
abs.	מָצוֹא		נִמְצֹא	מַצֵּא
Participle				
ms	מָצוּא / מֹצֵא (active)/(passive)	—	נִמְצָא	מְמַצֵּא

	Pual	Hiphil	Hophal	Hithpael
Perfect				
3ms	מֻצָּא	הִמְצִיא	הֻמְצָא	הִתְמַצֵּא
3fs	מֻצְּאָה	הִמְצִיאָה	הֻמְצְאָה	הִתְמַצְּאָה
2ms	מֻצֵּאתָ	הִמְצֵּאתָ	הֻמְצֵאתָ	הִתְמַצֵּאתָ
2fs	מֻצֵּאת	הִמְצֵאת	הֻמְצֵאת	הִתְמַצֵּאת
1cs	מֻצֵּאתִי	הִמְצֵּאתִי	הֻמְצֵּאתִי	הִתְמַצֵּאתִי
3cp	מֻצְּאוּ	הִמְצִיאוּ	הֻמְצְאוּ	הִתְמַצְּאוּ
2mp	מֻצֵּאתֶם	הִמְצֵאתֶם	הֻמְצֵאתֶם	הִתְמַצֵּאתֶם
2fp	מֻצֵּאתֶן	הִמְצֵאתֶן	הֻמְצֵאתֶן	הִתְמַצֵּאתֶן
1cp	מֻצֵּאנוּ	הִמְצֵּאנוּ	הֻמְצֵּאנוּ	הִתְמַצֵּאנוּ
Imperfect				
3ms	יְמֻצָּא	יַמְצִיא	יֻמְצָא	יִתְמַצֵּא
3fs	תְּמֻצָּא	תַּמְצִיא	תֻּמְצָא	תִּתְמַצֵּא
2ms	תְּמֻצָּא	תַּמְצִיא	תֻּמְצָא	תִּתְמַצֵּא
2fs	תְּמֻצְּאִי	תַּמְצִיאִי	תֻּמְצְאִי	תִּתְמַצְּאִי
1cs	אֲמֻצָּא	אַמְצִיא	אֻמְצָא	אֶתְמַצֵּא
3mp	יְמֻצְּאוּ	יַמְצִיאוּ	יֻמְצְאוּ	יִתְמַצְּאוּ
3fp	תְּמֻצֶּאנָה	תַּמְצֶאנָה	תֻּמְצֶאנָה	תִּתְמַצֶּאנָה
2mp	תְּמֻצְּאוּ	תַּמְצִיאוּ	תֻּמְצְאוּ	תִּתְמַצְּאוּ
2fp	תְּמֻצֶּאנָה	תַּמְצֶאנָה	תֻּמְצֶאנָה	תִּתְמַצֶּאנָה
1cp	נְמֻצָּא	נַמְצִיא	נֻמְצָא	נִתְמַצֵּא
Imperative				
ms	—	הַמְצֵא	—	הִתְמַצֵּא
fs	—	הַמְצִיאִי	—	הִתְמַצְּאִי
mp	—	הַמְצִיאוּ	—	הִתְמַצְּאוּ
fp	—	הַמְצֶאנָה	—	הִתְמַצֶּאנָה
Infinitive				
cstr.	wanting	הַמְצִיא	wanting	הִתְמַצֵּא
abs.	wanting	הַמְצֵא	wanting	הִתְמַצֵּא
Participle				
ms	מְמֻצָּא	מַמְצִיא	מֻמְצָא	מִתְמַצֵּא

PARADIGM 12
Lamedh–He Verb

	Qal	Niphal	Piel
Perfect			
3ms	גָּלָה	נִגְלָה	גִּלָּה
3fs	גָּלְתָה	נִגְלְתָה	גִּלְּתָה
2ms	גָּלִיתָ	נִגְלֵיתָ	גִּלִּיתָ
2fs	גָּלִית	נִגְלֵית	גִּלִּית
1cs	גָּלִיתִי	נִגְלֵיתִי	גִּלִּיתִי
3cp	גָּלוּ	נִגְלוּ	גִּלּוּ
2mp	גְּלִיתֶם	נִגְלֵיתֶם	גִּלִּיתֶם
2fp	גְּלִיתֶן	נִגְלֵיתֶן	גִּלִּיתֶן
1cp	גָּלִינוּ	נִגְלֵינוּ	גִּלִּינוּ
Imperfect			
3ms	יִגְלֶה	יִגָּלֶה	יְגַלֶּה
3fs	תִּגְלֶה	תִּגָּלֶה	תְּגַלֶּה
2ms	תִּגְלֶה	תִּגָּלֶה	תְּגַלֶּה
2fs	תִּגְלִי	תִּגָּלִי	תְּגַלִּי
1cs	אֶגְלֶה	אֶגָּלֶה	אֲגַלֶּה
3mp	יִגְלוּ	יִגָּלוּ	יְגַלּוּ
3fp	תִּגְלֶינָה	תִּגָּלֶינָה	תְּגַלֶּינָה
2mp	תִּגְלוּ	תִּגָּלוּ	תְּגַלּוּ
2fp	תִּגְלֶינָה	תִּגָּלֶינָה	תְּגַלֶּינָה
1cp	נִגְלֶה	נִגָּלֶה	נְגַלֶּה
Imperative			
ms	גְּלֵה	הִגָּלֵה	גַּלֵּה
fs	גְּלִי	הִגָּלִי	גַּלִּי
mp	גְּלוּ	הִגָּלוּ	גַּלּוּ
fp	גְּלֶינָה	הִגָּלֶינָה	גַּלֶּינָה
Infinitive			
cstr.	גְּלוֹת	הִגָּלוֹת	גַּלּוֹת
abs.	גָּלֹה	נִגְלֹה and הִגָּלֵה	גַּלֹּה and גַּלֵּה
Participle			
ms	גֹּלֶה / גָּלוּי	נִגְלֶה	מְגַלֶּה
	(active)/(passive)		

	Pual	Hiphil	Hophal	Hithpael
Perfect				
3ms	גֻּלָּה	הִגְלָה	הָגְלָה	הִתְגַּלָּה
3fs	גֻּלְּתָה	הִגְלְתָה	הָגְלְתָה	הִתְגַּלְּתָה
2ms	גֻּלֵּיתָ	הִגְלֵיתָ	הָגְלֵיתָ	הִתְגַּלֵּיתָ
2fs	גֻּלֵּית	הִגְלֵית	הָגְלֵית	הִתְגַּלֵּית
1cs	גֻּלֵּיתִי	הִגְלֵיתִי	הָגְלֵיתִי	הִתְגַּלֵּיתִי
3cp	גֻּלּוּ	הִגְלוּ	הָגְלוּ	הִתְגַּלּוּ
2mp	גֻּלֵּיתֶם	הִגְלֵיתֶם	הָגְלֵיתֶם	הִתְגַּלֵּיתֶם
2fp	גֻּלֵּיתֶן	הִגְלֵיתֶן	הָגְלֵיתֶן	הִתְגַּלֵּיתֶן
1cp	גֻּלֵּינוּ	הִגְלֵינוּ	הָגְלֵינוּ	הִתְגַּלֵּינוּ
Imperfect				
3ms	יְגֻלֶּה	יַגְלֶה	יָגְלֶה	יִתְגַּלֶּה
3fs	תְּגֻלֶּה	תַּגְלֶה	תָּגְלֶה	תִּתְגַּלֶּה
2ms	תְּגֻלֶּה	תַּגְלֶה	תָּגְלֶה	תִּתְגַּלֶּה
2fs	תְּגֻלִּי	תַּגְלִי	תָּגְלִי	תִּתְגַּלִּי
1cs	אֲגֻלֶּה	אַגְלֶה	אָגְלֶה	אֶתְגַּלֶּה
3mp	יְגֻלּוּ	יַגְלוּ	יָגְלוּ	יִתְגַּלּוּ
3fp	תְּגֻלֶּינָה	תַּגְלֶינָה	תָּגְלֶינָה	תִּתְגַּלֶּינָה
2mp	תְּגֻלּוּ	תַּגְלוּ	תָּגְלוּ	תִּתְגַּלּוּ
2fp	תְּגֻלֶּינָה	תַּגְלֶינָה	תָּגְלֶינָה	תִּתְגַּלֶּינָה
1cp	נְגֻלֶּה	נַגְלֶה	נָגְלֶה	נִתְגַּלֶּה
Imperative				
ms	—	הַגְלֵה	—	הִתְגַּלֵּה
fs	—	הַגְלִי	—	הִתְגַּלִּי
mp	—	הַגְלוּ	—	הִתְגַּלּוּ
fp	—	הַגְלֶינָה	—	הִתְגַּלֶּינָה
Infinitive				
cstr.	wanting	הַגְלוֹת	הָגְלוֹת	הִתְגַּלּוֹת
abs.	wanting	הַגְלֵה	הָגְלֵה	הִתְגַּלֵּה
Participle				
ms	מְגֻלֶּה	מַגְלֶה	מָגְלֶה	מִתְגַּלֶּה

PARADIGM 13

Geminate Verb

	Qal				Niphal
Perfect					
3ms	סָבַב		תַּם		נָסַב
3fs	סָבְבָה		תַּמָּה		נָסַבָּה
2ms	סַבּוֹתָ		תַּמּוֹתָ		נְסַבּוֹתָ
2fs	סַבּוֹת		תַּמּוֹת		נְסַבּוֹת
1cs	סַבּוֹתִי		תַּמּוֹתִי		נְסַבּוֹתִי
3cp	סָבְבוּ		תַּמּוּ		נָסַבּוּ
2mp	סַבּוֹתֶם		תַּמּוֹתֶם		נְסַבּוֹתֶם
2fp	סַבּוֹתֶן		תַּמּוֹתֶן		נְסַבּוֹתֶן
1cp	סַבּוֹנוּ		תַּמּוֹנוּ		נְסַבּוֹנוּ
Imperfect					
3ms	יָסֹב	יִסֹּב	יֵתַם	יִתַּם	יִסַּב
3fs	תָּסֹב	תִּסֹּב	תֵּתַם	תִּתַּם	תִּסַּב
2ms	תָּסֹב	תִּסֹּב	תֵּתַם	תִּתַּם	תִּסַּב
2fs	תָּסֹבִּי	תִּסֹּבִי	תֵּתַּמִּי	תִּתַּמִּי	תִּסַּבִּי
1cs	אָסֹב	אֶסֹּב	אֵתַם	אֶתַּם	אֶסַּב
3mp	יָסֹבּוּ	יִסֹּבוּ	יֵתַּמּוּ	יִתַּמּוּ	יִסַּבּוּ
3fp	תְּסֻבֶּינָה	תִּסֹּבְנָה	תְּתֻמֶּינָה	תִּתַּמְנָה	תִּסַּבֶּינָה
2mp	תָּסֹבּוּ	תִּסֹּבוּ	תֵּתַּמּוּ	תִּתַּמּוּ	תִּסַּבּוּ
2fp	תְּסֻבֶּינָה	תִּסֹּבְנָה	תְּתֻמֶּינָה	תִּתַּמְנָה	תִּסַּבֶּינָה
1cp	נָסֹב	נִסֹּב	נֵתַם	נִתַּם	נִסַּב
Imperative					
ms	סֹב		תַּם		הִסַּב
fs	סֹבִּי		תַּמִּי		הִסַּבִּי
mp	סֹבּוּ		תַּמּוּ		הִסַּבּוּ
fp	סֻבֶּינָה		תַּמֶּינָה		הִסַּבֶּינָה
Infinitive					
cstr.	סְבֹב and סֹב		תֹּם		הִסֵּב
abs.	סָבוֹב		תָּמוֹם		הִסֵּב and הִסוֹב
Participle					
ms	סָבוּב / סֹבֵב		—		נָסָב
	(active/passive)				

	Hiphil	Hophal
Perfect		
3ms	הֵסֵב	הוּסַב
3fs	הֵסֵּבָּה	הוּסַבָּה
2ms	הֲסִבּוֹתָ	הוּסַבּוֹתָ
2fs	הֲסִבּוֹת	הוּסַבּוֹת
1cs	הֲסִבּוֹתִי	הוּסַבּוֹתִי
3cp	הֵסֵּבּוּ	הוּסַבּוּ
2mp	הֲסִבּוֹתֶם	הוּסַבּוֹתֶם
2fp	הֲסִבּוֹתֶן	הוּסַבּוֹתֶן
1cp	הֲסִבּוֹנוּ	הוּסַבּוֹנוּ

Imperfect				
3ms	יָסֵב	יַסֵּב	יוּסַב	יֻסַּב
3fs	תָּסֵב	תַּסֵּב	תּוּסַב	תֻּסַּב
2ms	תָּסֵב	תַּסֵּב	תּוּסַב	תֻּסַּב
2fs	תָּסֵבִּי	תַּסֵּבִּי	תּוּסַבִּי	תֻּסַּבִּי
1cs	אָסֵב	אַסֵּב	אוּסַב	אֻסַּב
3mp	יָסֵבּוּ	יַסֵּבּוּ	יוּסַבּוּ	יֻסַּבּוּ
3fp	תְּסִבֶּינָה	תַּסֵּבְּנָה	תּוּסַבֶּינָה	תֻּסַּבְּנָה
2mp	תָּסֵבּוּ	תַּסֵּבּוּ	תּוּסַבּוּ	תֻּסַּבּוּ
2fp	תְּסִבֶּינָה	תַּסֵּבְּנָה	תּוּסַבֶּינָה	תֻּסַּבְּנָה
1cp	נָסֵב	נַסֵּב	נוּסַב	נֻסַּב

Imperative	Hiphil	Hophal
ms	הָסֵב	—
fs	הָסֵבִּי	—
mp	הָסֵבּוּ	—
fp	הֲסִבֶּינָה	—

Infinitive	Hiphil	Hophal
cstr.	הָסֵב	wanting
abs.	הָסֵב	הוּסֵב

Participle	Hiphil	Hophal
ms	מֵסֵב	מוּסַב

Note that the Poel, Poal and Hithpoel stems of geminate roots conjugate the same as Polel, Polal and Hithpolel stems of hollow roots (see Paradigm 9): for example, יְסוֹבֵב, סוֹבַב, מְסוֹבֵב.

SUBJECT INDEX
(numbers refer to sections, unless otherwise specified)